The One by Whom Scandal Comes

Studies in Violence, Mimesis, and Culture

The One by Whom Scandal Comes

René Girard

Translated by M. B. DeBevoise

Michigan State University Press · *East Lansing*

♾ The paper used in this publication meets the minimum requirements of ANSI/NISO
Z39.48-1992 (R 1997) (Permanence of Paper).

 Michigan State University Press
East Lansing, Michigan 48823-5245

Printed and bound in the United States of America.

20 19 18 17 16 15 14   1 2 3 4 5 6 7 8 9 10

LIBRARY OF CONGRESS CATALOGING-IN-PUBLICATION DATA
Girard, René, 1923–
[Celui par qui le scandale arrive. English]
The one by whom scandal comes / René Girard ; translated by M. B. DeBevoise.
pages cm.— (Studies in violence, mimesis, and culture series)
Includes bibliographical references and index.
ISBN 978-1-60917-399-9 (ebook)—ISBN 978-1-61186-109-9 (pbk. : alk. paper)
1. Violence—Religious aspects. I. Title.
BL65.V55G56513 2014
261.7—dc23
2013012137

Book design and composition by Charlie Sharp, Sharp Des!gns, Lansing, Michigan
Cover design by David Drummond, Salamander Design, www.salamanderhill.com
Cover art is *Judith and Holofernes,* 1612–21 (oil on canvas), Gentileschi, Artemisia (1597–
c. 1651) / Galleria degli Uffizi, Florence, Italy / Alinari / The Bridgeman Art Library. Used
with permission.

**g green
press
INITIATIVE** Michigan State University Press is a member of the Green Press Initiative
and is committed to developing and encouraging ecologically responsible
publishing practices. For more information about the Green Press Initiative and the use of
recycled paper in book publishing, please visit *www.greenpressinitiative.org.*

Visit Michigan State University Press at *www.msupress.org*

Contents

vii   A Note on the Translation

ix   Preface

PART I. AGAINST RELATIVISM

3   CHAPTER 1. Violence and Reciprocity

21   CHAPTER 2. Noble Savages and Others

33   CHAPTER 3. Mimetic Theory and Theology

PART 2. THE OTHER SIDE OF MYTH

49   CHAPTER 4. I See Satan Fall Like Lightning

57   CHAPTER 5. Scandal and Conversion

67   CHAPTER 6. I Do Not Pray for the World

75   CHAPTER 7. The Catholic Church and the Modern World

85   CHAPTER 8. Hominization and Natural Selection

93   CHAPTER 9. A Stumbling Block to Jews, Foolishness to Gentiles

103 CHAPTER 10. Lévi-Strauss on Collective Murder

113 CHAPTER 11. Positivists and Deconstructionists

127 CHAPTER 12. How Should Mimetic Theory Be Applied?

131 Notes

137 Index

A Note on the Translation

In the matter of scriptural citation I have quoted from the New American Bible, the verse numbering of which sometimes differs from Protestant bibles, and added a number of notes identifying various passages alluded to in the text. I have, however, followed the author in preferring the New King James Version's rendering of the famous phrase from Matthew 12:26, "Satan casts out Satan."

A modest amount of bibliographical information has been added, as well as some biographical detail in the case of persons who may not be well known to general readers. Several minor errors of fact have been silently corrected as well.

I am grateful to Professor William A. Johnsen for his careful scrutiny of a draft version.

Preface

The one by whom scandal comes—a rather grand and somewhat incriminating title, suggested by Maria Stella Barberi, who assures me that in proposing it to Benoît Chantre at Éditions Desclée de Brouwer in Paris she did not have the author of the present work in mind! She was inspired, she says, by the topics I discuss, which bear on all the most controversial points of mimetic theory.

In the three essays that make up the first part of this book, as well as in the conversation with Maria Stella Barberi that comprises the second part, I respond to objections that have long been brought against my work, as well as to questions never treated, or only lightly touched upon, in my earlier books. At the same time I continue to explore a number of themes that are dear to my heart, giving more specific and more modern examples than I have done in the past.

In the first essay, after a brief mimetic analysis of contemporary terrorism, I take up the problem of conflicts that frequently erupt among persons who are indifferent to one another, whom desire neither brings closer together nor pulls apart. These conflicts—even (and above all) the most pointless ones of their kind—are also mimetic, for they are rooted, like so many others, in a widely shared desire for something that cannot be shared. Mimeticism is the very substance of all manner of human relations.

In the second essay I turn to the question of ethnocentrism, for which my anthropology is often reproached. Those who protest against "Western ethnocentrism" imagine themselves to owe nothing to the West, since after all they rage furiously against it. But in fact theirs is the most Western perspective of all, more Western than that of their adversaries.

Not only is the revolt against ethnocentrism an invention of the West, it cannot be found outside the West. Its first great literary success was Montaigne's famous essay "Of Cannibals," now more than four hundred years old. Montaigne's anti-Western rhetoric, not always very sincere, was the opening salvo in a long war conducted exclusively against the ethnocentrism of the West. This struggle produced its finest masterpieces in the eighteenth century. Then, following a lull, it resumed after the Second World War with even greater ferocity.

The most recent phase is marked by a renunciation of the elegance and wit of our illustrious ancestors in favor of very twentieth-century neologisms, among them the graceless word "ethnocentrism" itself. In this way the rococo bibelots of the century of the Enlightenment have come to be coated with a rather thick layer of varnish. Whereas Montesquieu tried to imagine what it would be like to be Persian, our contemporaries ponderously rail against the West's preoccupation with itself. At bottom, however, the debate has scarcely changed.

There is nothing illegitimate about the debate itself. Western culture is quite obviously ethnocentric. But it is no more ethnocentric than any other, even if its ethnocentrism has been more cruelly effective on account of its power. There is no denying its cruelty. But why shouldn't we also recognize an equally obvious and irrefutable historical fact, namely, that unlike all other cultures, which have always been unashamedly ethnocentric, we in the West have always been simultaneously ourselves and our own enemy. We are at once His Majesty and the opponents of His Majesty. We condemn what we are, or what we believe ourselves to be, with an ardor that seldom amounts to very much, but at least we try. What is happening today is yet another example of the passion for self-criticism, which exists only among persons influenced by Judeo-Christian civilization.

The third essay in the first part of the book, written in honor of the Swiss

Roman Catholic theologian Raymund Schwager, has never been published in French or English. In recognizing the soundness of the Christian use of the term "sacrifice," it attempts to rectify the error of the so-called anti-sacrificial argument I made in my first writings on this subject, especially in *Things Hidden Since the Foundation of the World*. This rectification, though it is by no means a trivial matter on the theological level, changes absolutely nothing with regard to mimetic anthropology. It brings my perspective into closer alignment with traditional theologies, as I have always wished. Schwager himself understands my purpose, unlike other theologians who insist on subjecting me to the equivalent of a final exam and then delight in flunking me, even though they have long ceased to subject either themselves or other Christians to a trial of this sort. It is a very great honor they have done me.

The questions raised in my conversation with Maria Stella Barberi, which took place in two sessions (the first on 11 October 2000 in Paris and the second a month later, on 10 November, in Agen), are too numerous to be reviewed in a brief introduction. I will mention only one, which I had never considered before and which, owing to the prominent place given it here, highlights the anthropological emphasis of the book as a whole. It involves the relationship between mimetic theory and the dominant perspective of the second half of the twentieth century, due to Claude Lévi-Strauss.

In the first essay I sketched a critique of structuralism. Lévi-Strauss's immense ingenuity notwithstanding, an anthropology built solely on "differences" that takes no account of identity is inevitably incomplete, mutilated. In concentrating its attention exclusively on social order, it neglects the disorder and the crises that, as the great political theorist Carl Schmitt quite clearly saw, the social sciences must deal with if they are to become truly scientific. This is what mimetic theory tries to do, although not, of course, in the spirit of Carl Schmitt.

In my conversation with Maria Stella Barberi I speak again of Lévi-Strauss and of the influence that his books had on my thinking. I continue to disagree with structural anthropology on more things than not, but that does not prevent me from remaining a great admirer of the work of its founder, one of the finest scholarly achievements of the twentieth century—the anthropological century par excellence. Lévi-Strauss, without knowing it, taught me anthropology.

I mention also his very low opinion of mimetic theory. Although he names neither the theory nor its author, it seems clear that I am the person whom he has in mind when he repudiates any attempt to relaunch the absurd enterprise begun by Freud in *Totem and Taboo*. Expressions such as "scapegoat" and "founding murder" make Lévi-Strauss's skin crawl. They play a central role in my work, it is true—but not in the sense imagined by Lévi-Strauss, who knows nothing of me, I fear, apart from what rumor has to tell him. It appears to have told him scarcely anything more than these two, or possibly three expressions, which he repeats with a pitying smile.

The view of my work he ignorantly endorses fails to do justice to the idea of the "scapegoat" that I develop (which in fact is how most people think of it, in very simple and yet very profound terms). Lévi-Strauss would have it that I am a disciple of the later Freud. As I make clear in my conversation with Maria Stella Barberi, his view of me, which was immediately adopted by French ethnologists, is based on a complete misunderstanding of mimetic theory.

The present book has an unmistakably polemical character. I make a point of arguing against the obligatory relativism of our age, which in turn is inseparable from structuralism and deconstruction. But my purpose is not merely polemical. This book is above all an account of the present state of research that I have been conducting for more than forty years now. It marks an important step forward in a line of inquiry that, I hope, will never be exhausted.

I am grateful to Maria Stella Barberi for her questions and comments, as learned and sophisticated as they are pertinent. The present book owes not only its title to her, but also the form in which its chapters are presented. She is the editor of another book as well, a twin to this one since it will come out at the same time with the same publisher, *La spirale mimétique: Dix-huit leçons sur René Girard*. My thanks also to Giuseppe Fornari for his help, always appreciated, and to Joseph Bosshard. Finally, I am indebted to Benoît Chantre for his contagious enthusiasm, and to the whole team at Éditions Desclée de Brouwer. Without the devoted efforts of all these people, this book would never have appeared.

PART 1

Against Relativism

CHAPTER 1

Violence and Reciprocity

How shall we find the concord of this discord?
—Shakespeare, *A Midsummer Night's Dream* (Act V, scene i)

Why is there so much violence in our midst? No question is more debated today. And none produces more disappointing answers.

In the past, when people talked about the threats facing humanity, they always mentioned human violence, but it came after other perils that seemed to them still more formidable: destiny, the gods, nature, perhaps also the ferocious beasts that painters and illustrators until not so very long ago imagined to be even more enormous and more frightening than they really were. We may smile on being reminded of this, but in a way that suggests nostalgia more than amusement. Of all the threats presently looming over us, the most dreadful one, as we well realize, the only real threat, is ourselves. This truth becomes more striking every day, for every day our violence grows greater.

With the end of the Cold War, the risks of cataclysmic war receded and pacifists rejoiced. Nevertheless there was a sense of foreboding, that another titanic contest had merely been postponed. It had long been said, though no one really believed it, that terrorism would take the place of traditional warfare. It was hard to see how terrorism could be as terrifying as the prospect of a nuclear exchange between superpowers. Today we see.

Violence seems be to be escalating in a way that may be likened to the spread of a fire or an epidemic. The great mythic images rise up again before our eyes, as if violence had rediscovered a very ancient and rather mysterious form, a swirling vortex in which the most acute kinds of violence merge into one. There is one kind of violence, the kind found in families and in schools, especially in America, where teenagers slaughter their classmates. And then there is the kind of violence that is now seen throughout the world, a terrorism without limits or boundaries that heralds an age of wars of extermination against civil populations. We seem to be hurtling toward a moment when all mankind will be confronted with the reality of its own violence.

So long as globalization was slow in coming, everyone hoped and prayed that it would come soon. The unity of the world's nations was one of the great triumphalist themes of modernism. World's fairs were staged in its honor, one after another. Now that globalization is here, however, it arouses more anxiety than pride. The erasing of differences may not portend the era of universal reconciliation that everyone confidently expected.

There are two main modern approaches to violence. The first is political and philosophical. It holds that human beings are naturally good and ascribes anything that contradicts this assumption to the imperfections of society, to the oppression of the people by the ruling classes. The second is biological. Within the animal kingdom, which is naturally peaceable, only the human race is truly capable of violence. Freud spoke of a death instinct. Today we seek to identify the genes responsible for aggression.

These two approaches have proved to be sterile. For years now I have argued for a third approach, one that is both very new and very old. When I speak of it a certain interest is awakened, only to be immediately replaced by skepticism once I pronounce the key word of my hypothesis: *imitation*.

Biologically determined appetites and needs, which are common to both men and animals, and unchanging since they bear upon fixed objects, stand in contrast to *desire* and *passion*, which are exclusively human. Passion, intense desire, is born the moment our vague longings are trained on a *model* that suggests to us what we should desire, typically in desiring the model itself. This model may be society as a whole, but often it is an individual whom we admire. Everything that humanity endows with prestige it transforms into a model. This is true not only of children and adolescents, but also of adults.

In observing people around us we quickly perceive that mimetic desire, or desirous imitation, dominates not only the smallest details of our everyday behavior, but also the most important choices of our lives, the choice of a spouse, of a career, even the meaning that we give to our existence. What we call desire or passion is not mimetic accidentally, or from time to time, but is mimetic unavoidably, all the time. Far from being the most personal emotion there is, our desire comes from others. Nothing could be more social.

Imitation plays an important role among the higher mammals, notably among our closest relatives, the great apes. It becomes more powerful still among human beings, and it is the principal reason why we are more intelligent, but also more combative and more violent, than all the other mammals. Imitation is human intelligence in its most dynamic aspect. It goes beyond animality, then, but it also causes us to lose animal equilibrium; indeed we may fall very far below those whom we used to call our "lower brothers." Once I desire what a model fairly close to me in time and space desires, with a view to bringing the object I covet through him within my grasp, I try to take this object away from him—and so rivalry between the two of us becomes inevitable.

This is mimetic rivalry. It can become extraordinarily acute. Curiously, however, even though mimetic rivalry is responsible for the frequency and intensity of human conflict, no one ever speaks of it. It does everything possible to conceal itself, even from the eyes of those who are party to it, and generally it succeeds.

Internecine conflict can lead to violent death, the prospect of which nevertheless does not deter human combatants. Mimetic rivalry is observed in other mammals, but there it is relatively weak and almost always interrupted before becoming fatal. It produces dominance patterns that, generally speaking, are more stable than human relations, which are subject to a quite particular form of mimeticism.

When an imitator attempts to snatch away from his model the object of their common desire, the model resists, of course, and desire becomes more intense *on both sides*. The model becomes the imitator of his imitator, and vice versa. Their roles are exchanged and reflected in an ever more perfect mutual imitation that heightens the resemblance between the antagonists. One must not see this as a simple mirror effect, in the Lacanian sense, but as a real action that alters our relations with others and ends up pushing each of us in the very direction we imagined ourselves to have avoided by opposing our model: the greater the resemblance between mimetic rivals, the more closely they identify with each other. This process of undifferentiation is nothing other than the *ever greater violence* that threatens us at the present hour.

The great Greek philosophers, and particularly Plato and Aristotle, recognized the cardinal importance of imitation in human behavior, but they misunderstood the nature of mimetic rivalry. The case of Plato is especially striking. He creates an ontology in which reality as a whole is imitative, and yet human imitation is held to be deficient, even dangerous. Plato pretends to disdain imitation, but plainly he fears it, even if he never actually says what it is he dreads. This fear is connected, of course, with rivalrous relations that are mostly unidentified as well.

Aristotle, for his part, seems scarcely even to suspect that the cause of violence might be found in imitation, which he takes to be unproblematic. Man, he says, is the most mimetic of all animals. He also says there is nothing we like so much as imitation. He is right in both cases, but, like Plato, he fails to detect the source of violence in imitation. He sees quite clearly that friendship often leads to rivalry, but he limits rivalry to an aristocratic form of emulation that involves only virtuous behaviors. Aristotle never considers the situation of those who, unlike him, are neither aristocrats nor more gifted than others. He does not fear competition. He sees the essential problem but manages with great elegance to avoid coming to terms with it.

The Platonist ontology of imitation and the philosophical and psychological conception that, following Aristotle, limits imitation to external behaviors, to ways of acting or speaking, must therefore be rejected. In both cases, the essential point is evaded. Modern romantic philosophy despises imitation, and the nearer one comes to the present the more pronounced this scorn becomes. Oddly, it is based on the supposed inability of imitators to challenge their models. Mimeticism is supposed to be a renunciation of true individuality, with the result that the individual is beaten down by "others" and forced to yield to the common opinion.

Passive, submissive imitation does exist, but hatred of conformity and extreme individualism are no less imitative. Today they constitute a negative conformism that is more formidable than the positive version. More and more, it seems to me, modern individualism assumes the form of a desperate denial of the fact that, through mimetic desire, each of us seeks to impose his will upon his fellow man, whom he professes to love but more often despises.

When we imitate others, as it is usually said, we are being unfaithful to ourselves. The outstanding characteristic of imitators is not violence; it is passivity, herd behavior. This is what I call the romantic lie, which in the twentieth century was most famously described by Martin Heidegger. In *Being and Time*, the "inauthentic" self is identical with the "they" (*das Man*) of collective irresponsibility. Passive and conformist imitation abandons the struggle to affirm one's true personality. It is opposed to the authentic self of the philosopher himself, who has no fear of going to war against adversaries who are worthy of him, in the Heracleitean spirit of *pólemos*—the violence that is "father of all and king of all." Struggle and conflict are seen as proofs of authenticity, of a will to power in the Nietzschean sense of the term.

I maintain that passion and desire are never authentic in the Heidegger-ean sense. They do not emerge from the depths of our being; we always borrow them from others. Far from seeing conflict as a sign of mastery, as Heidegger does, we must see it as exactly the opposite, a confirmation of the mimetic nature of our desires.

Individualists, as all of us imagine ourselves to be, have the impression that they no longer imitate anyone once they have forcibly overcome their model. Far from being incompatible with imitation, Heracleitean violence is an idealized version of mimetic rivalry. A more penetrating critical eye detects in it the romantic lie of which I just spoke.

To understand our current predicament we must first look inside ourselves— and no less closely than we must then look at the world around us. Our world is filled with competition, frenzied ambition in every domain. Each of us is acquainted with the spirit of competition. This spirit is not a bad thing in and of itself. Its influence has long been felt in personal relations within the dominant classes. Subsequently it spread throughout the whole of society, to the point that today it has more or less openly triumphed in every part of the world. In Western nations, and above all in the United States, it animates not only economic and financial life, but scientific research and intellectual life as well. Despite the tension and the unrest it brings, these nations are inclined on the whole to congratulate themselves for having embraced the spirit of competition, for its positive effects are considerable. Not the least of these is the impressive wealth it has brought a large part of the population. No one, or almost no one, any longer thinks of forgoing rivalry, since it allows us to go on dreaming of a still more glittering and prosperous future than the recent past. Our world seems to us the most desirable one there ever was, especially when we compare it to life in nations that have not enjoyed the same prosperity.

On both sides there is a reliance on ancestral traditions to explain phenomena that, to the contrary, are rooted quite obviously in the loss of these traditions—a loss that has remained uncompensated until the present day. The hatred of the West and of everything that it represents arises not because its spirit is really foreign to the peoples of the third world, nor because they are really opposed to the "progress" that we embody, but because the competitive spirit is as familiar to them as it is to ourselves. Far from turning away from the West, they cannot prevent themselves from imitating it, from adopting its values without admitting it to themselves. They are no less consumed than we are by the ideology of individual and collective success.

The rivalrous ideal that our example imposes on the whole planet cannot make us conquerors without there being uncountably many vanquished, uncountably many victims. It is hardly surprising, then, that this ideology should produce reactions among the vanquished that are very different from the ones it produces among the conquerors themselves. Above all it creates a fervent determination to utterly shatter the enormous competitive machine that the United States, closely followed by all the other nations of the West, has become, a source of immense personal and national humiliation.

People everywhere today are exposed to a contagion of violence that perpetuates cycles of vengeance. These interlocking episodes resemble each other, quite obviously, because they all imitate each other. This is why I say the true secret of conflict and violence is mimetic desire. Even if one admits that such desire and the fierce rivalries it generates are the cause of many conflicts, one may still think that there are other conflictual relations from which mimetic desire is absent, and that I exaggerate its role in making it the principal cause of human conflict. One may suspect me, in other words, of surrendering to the facile pleasures of reductionism.

There are many conflicts, small and large, which seem to have nothing to do with mimeticism, because desire plays no role in them. The least passionate human relations can also be riddled with violence. How can the mimetic conception I propose account for conflicts that break out, and are aggravated with disconcerting ease, among individuals who, it would appear, are neither separated nor drawn together by any common desire?

To reply to this objection, let us take the most insignificant example imaginable: you extend your hand to me and I, in return, extend my hand to you. Together we perform the harmless ritual of shaking hands. Faced with your extended hand, politeness requires that I extend mine. If, for whatever reason, I refuse to take part in the ritual, if I refuse to imitate you, how do you react? At once you withdraw your hand as well. You show a reticence toward me that is at least equal to, and probably a bit greater than, the reticence I have shown toward you.

We suppose that there is nothing more normal, more natural than this reaction, and yet a moment's reflection will reveal its paradoxical character. If I decline to shake your hand, if, in short, I refuse to imitate you, then you are now the one who imitates me, by reproducing my refusal, by copying me instead. Imitation, which usually expresses agreement in this case, now serves to confirm and strengthen disagreement. Once again, in other words, imitation triumphs. Here we see how rigorously, how implacably mutual imitation structures even the simplest human relations.

When the imitator becomes the model and the model the imitator, imitation is given new life by the attempt to deny it. When one of the two partners drops the torch of mimeticism, as it were, the other one catches it before it falls to the ground—not in order to preserve a continuity that is about to be broken, but to complete the rupture by replicating it, mimetically.

If a person B turns away from A, who extends his hand to him, A immediately takes offense and, in his turn, refuses to shake B's hand. In the context of the first refusal, the second one comes too late and risks going unperceived. A will therefore try to make it more visible by emphasizing it a bit, by very slightly overdoing it. Perhaps, more obviously still, he will turn his back on *B*. The thought of triggering a cycle of violent retaliation is far from his mind. He wants simply to make a point—to make *B* understand that the insulting character of his behavior has not escaped his attention.

What *A* interprets as a discourtesy, a deliberate slight, may be nothing more than a momentary distraction on the part of *B*, whose mind was on something else. And yet the idea that it may have been a conscious insult is less wounding to *A*'s vanity than the thought of being unnoticed, even for a moment. However miniscule the original misunderstanding, if *B* now tries to explain himself to *A*, the shadow suddenly cast over their encounter, so far from being dispelled, only grows darker.

The coolness that *A* displays toward him seems unjust to *B*, and in order to even accounts between them *B* will respond in the same way, only with an extra bit of coolness added for good measure. Neither *A* nor *B* wishes to quarrel, and yet the disagreement is there. Who is responsible?

The messages we send one another, as far as their content is concerned, are for the most part of little or no interest. As far as the emotional temperature of our relationships are concerned, however, they are ultra-sensitive thermometers, of much greater interest than the words actually exchanged. Language—"discourse," as it is known today—is much less important than current fashion would have it.

Most messages are sent out of pure politeness, and they are sent simply to be returned in the same form they were delivered. This is what in French is called *la bonne réciprocité*: we see ourselves as sending back a message without modifying it, or modifying it only slightly. In this way we hold up a mirror to our partner, to send back to him, for example, what seems to us to be coolness on his part. We are never the ones, we say to ourselves, who have taken a dangerous first step; it is always the other person.

Human relations are an unending exercise in mutual imitation—the essence of which is perfectly captured by a not wholly transparent word, *reciprocity*. A relationship may be benevolent and peaceable, or it may be malicious and belligerent. In either case, curiously, it does not cease to be reciprocal. This is very important for imitation, whose role is everywhere and always minimized.

Among animals, I think, there is very little mutual imitation. It is mainly in violent rivalry that reciprocity is manifest, though perhaps not even there, for in combat one has the impression that the adversaries do not really look at each other. The other is never present among animals as it is in the normal course of relations among human beings.

What characterizes human conflict is not the loss of reciprocity but the transition, imperceptible at first but then ever more rapid, from *good* to *bad* reciprocity. One scarcely notices this movement, and yet the least neglect, the least forgetfulness can have lastingly disruptive consequences. By contrast, movement in the opposite direction, from bad to good reciprocity, requires great vigilance and abnegation. It occurs more rarely.

As a general rule, the universality of mutual imitation escapes our notice. The only people who become aware of it in daily life are certain individuals who suffer from what the psychiatrist Henri Grivois calls "incipient psychosis." These individuals, typically adolescents, feel that they are constantly being imitated; some also feel that they themselves are imitators. The fact that most of us suspect no such thing (and, in order to remain normal, must not suspect it), is no less remarkable. It cannot help but modify to some extent our conceptions of the familiar and the novel, of the normal and the abnormal. The mechanistic character of mimeticism, which ordinarily goes unperceived, causes certain people who suddenly find themselves displaced, removed from their daily routine and their usual surroundings, to believe that they are the object of universal mimetic attention, and therefore the center of everyone else's world. Grivois calls this response *centrality*. Normality, on the other hand, means behaving like everyone else since this makes it possible to resist the illusion of being universally imitated.

Nothing is more common, then, than mutual imitation. Even in its most mechanistic form, it can generate the same type of conflict as rivalry that springs from mimetic desire. Concord is transformed into discord by a continual succession of small symmetrical ruptures, insensible aggravations that nullify each other, only then to reappear, strengthened. The principal cause of this is the tendency to overcompensate for the other's presumed hostility and, in so doing, perpetually reinforce it. The individuals who just a moment ago *were exchanging* pleasantries *are now exchanging* perfidious insinuations. And soon they *will be exchanging* insults, threats, even punches or gunshots—and all this, as I say, without reciprocity ever being disturbed.

If, finally, the adversaries manage to kill one another, it will have been in order to rid themselves of bad reciprocity, an ineradicable weed that then assumes the form of cycles of interminable violence. Vengeance succeeds in spanning generations and encompassing the world. It transcends time and space. One should not be surprised that in the ancient world vengeance was taken to be sacred.

It is important to recognize that all societies fear violence, even—indeed especially—if they do not think of it apart from religion. The unmistakable symptom of this fear is sameness, the state of being identical, undifferentiated. Twins were often brutally mistreated in many ancient societies, and in some cases put to death at birth, out of a fear that their extreme resemblance signified the advent of acute conflict.

Human culture consists essentially in an effort to prevent violence from being unleashed by separating and differentiating all those aspects of public and private life which, so long as they remain subject to the natural order of reciprocity, are at risk of lapsing into irremediable violence. Matrimonial prescriptions, for example, are ultimately reducible to a single rule, obliging nuclear families to give up what is uniquely theirs, in the first place female siblings and children, who threaten to unleash a destructive rivalry among those to whom they have belonged from the time of their birth.

These daughters and sisters whom we must not marry ourselves we hand over to our neighbors, so that they may marry them in our place. In exchange we receive their daughters and sisters, whom they must not marry themselves, and whom we marry in their place. The prohibition always falls on a family's nearest, most accessible possessions—which are therefore the ones likeliest to arouse conflict, the ones that are most dangerous from the point of view of their natural owners.

The same fear of violence among close relatives subsequently led to the exchange of goods of all kinds. In this way the crucial problem facing all cultures was broken up, fragmented, dispersed, and, in a sense, lost, led astray—forgotten in a maze of complicated rules and prohibitions, so that the underlying reciprocity, which always survives, cannot readily be rediscovered.

In several languages the word meaning "gift" also means "poison." In very, very remote times all gifts, I think, were poisoned: their original owners gave away only things that were a source of trouble and annoyance to them, and that they therefore sought to rid themselves of, in exchange for things that were just as useful but less bothersome, for the simple reason that they came from elsewhere. One makes a poisoned gift to a neighbor, in other words, not in order to make his life unbearable, but in order to make one's own life bearable. One seeks to get rid of anything that nourishes discord within oneself.

The reciprocal exchange of gifts proved to be a workable system because gifts that were poisoned to begin with became harmless once they were transferred to a foreign community. It was easier to live with others' women than with one's own—this, I think, is the origin of exchange. Marcel Mauss and many others wondered, without ever really answering their own question, why the most peaceable transactions always have a violent aspect to them, amounting sometimes to a very realistic simulation of acute conflict. It needs to be kept in mind that exchange, universal though it may be among human beings, is contrary to animal instinct, which always looks for satisfaction nearby, through things that are close at hand. A universal system of exchange, in the course of becoming established, must have provoked fearsome resistance at first. Owing to the extraordinary conservatism of rituals, traces of this violence are preserved in transactions that have come down to us from much later archaic systems.

Artificial differences served to protect archaic communities from bad reciprocity, which was always preceded and heralded by the unsettling pace of events associated with good reciprocity. In rural settings, until recently, customs survived—ancient habits, no doubt—that were meant to slow down the rhythm of even the most ordinary kinds of exchange. At the beginning of the twentieth century in France, for example, in the mountains of Auvergne, a conscious attempt was made to avoid conducting business too rapidly. If someone looking to buy a calf at the village fair took out his money too quickly, the seller invited him first for a drink at the café next door, in order to delay by a little (though not by too much, of course) the *settling of accounts*. The ambiguity of this expression, "settling of accounts," illuminates the fear provoked by a kind of reciprocity, abrupt enough to begin with, that threatens to be too sudden.

I understand the French word *différence* in the dual sense given it by

Jacques Derrida: on the one hand, non-identity in space, the *differentiating* of sameness; and, on the other, non-coincidence in time, the *deferring* of simultaneity. Difference and deferral are what make it possible, if not to destroy, then at least to disguise an indestructible reciprocity, to delay it by putting the greatest possible interval between the moments of which it is composed, an interval in both time and space, in the hope that the reciprocity of exchange will go unnoticed. One tries, in other words, to forget what is similar, identical; literally, to lose it, to lead it astray in a maze of differences so complicated, and of deferrals so prolonged, that one will no longer be able to find one's bearings.

Claude Lévi-Strauss was the first to formulate cultural rules in terms of differences. This was a very valuable step forward, but it fell short of what is needed if we are to understand culture in its full complexity. Differences must be situated in their real context, which is to say mimetic relations and their irrepressible power of undifferentiation, their power to reduce differences to sameness. Lévi-Strauss's principle is meaningful only by virtue of the resistance, never wholly successful, that cultures mount against identity, which is always perceived to be intrusive and menacing.

The idea of difference is not enough by itself. The contortions to which we have submitted in order to conceal this truth from ourselves will not manage to disguise forever the impossibility of constructing a coherent anthropology on the basis of differences alone. The current absolutism of difference is an absurdity, but not just any absurdity. It is an absurdity prepared long ago by the overly narrow and twisted conception that modern anthropology formed of its subject matter. In restricting itself to the study of cultural rules alone, without concerning itself with the context in which differences come to be situated, the human reality of violence ended up being erased.

Almost all ethnologists are relativists. They are persuaded that nothing in human cultures transcends the infinite diversity of rules, of permanently different differences. Difference is all there is, they triumphantly assert. They do not recall that they are the ones who resolved from the very beginning to neglect human relations, leaving this subject to whomever really thought it was worth studying—as if it could not possibly be worth their time! And because they have forgotten what they themselves had decided in the first place, they mistake their defacement of anthropology for an ultimate and conclusive discovery.

It is not difference that dominates the world, but the obliteration of difference by mimetic reciprocity, which itself, being truly universal, shows the relativism of perpetual difference to be an illusion. Reciprocity is always there from the beginning of every culture; and it is always there afterward, reappearing in its bad, violent form to put an end to every culture. Reciprocated violence, in other words, is the thing that causes cultures to perish, to fall back into the chaos from which they came. Mimetic theory reveals the true reason for the cyclical conceptions one finds among the Hindus and the pre-Socratic philosophers. Anaximander's famous phrases remain the best statement of this view of the universe:

> [T]he source from which existing things derive their existence is also that to which they return at their destruction, according to necessity; for they give justice and make reparation to one another for their injustice, according to the arrangement of Time.[1]

Modernism triumphed by deliberately going against the tide of human history. It was the first conception of the world since ancient times to resolutely take the side of reciprocity and identity against difference. In opposition to the perceived injustice of archaic and traditional religious hierarchies, modernism boldly championed equality and reciprocity in its good form. The whole philosophy of difference of which I have just spoken is only a recent and partial reaction to the fundamental dynamism that has characterized Western culture from well before the time of the French and American revolutions.

We are mistaken to bemoan our chronic propensity to violence without seeing its positive side. The fragility and instability of our relations with one another are the indispensable foundation not only of the worst part of our nature as human beings, but also of the best. If our relations with one another could not go wrong, they could not be put right. For true love to be possible, there must be hatred as well.

Modernism's wager is that good reciprocity will win out in the end. And indeed modern societies have shown themselves capable of absorbing large doses of everything that archaic and traditional societies wisely rejected, for they could not have tolerated, without perishing, everything that we tolerate still today. But no one can say what will happen tomorrow. Our future as a race will not unfold without great difficulties, without extraordinary tensions and turmoil. The recent spasms of violence we have witnessed are undoubtedly the most terrible in the whole of human history. But they cannot all be blamed on the triumph of modernism.

This is a vast subject that I can do no more than touch on very briefly. I shall therefore limit myself to the observation that our world has already done away with archaic and traditional differences, and in particular all the bloody sacrifices that were made for the purpose of reinvigorating these differences. But it has conserved, and actually multiplied, rites of good reciprocity found in the archaic world that were meant to block the tendency of peaceful relations to turn violent. More than ever before we devote ourselves to elaborate expressions of friendship, parties and celebrations, and the giving of expensive gifts on a more or less regular basis.

Nowadays, in a world traumatized by perpetual change, one observes a spontaneous tendency to lengthen the old formulas of politeness, in an unconscious effort, it seems to me, to make them more potent. Among English speakers, for example, "Have a good day" more and more often replaces the traditional but nebulous "Goodbye." In France, especially in Paris, taxi drivers amiably lengthen the somewhat offhand "Bonjour, bonsoir" into "Bonne soirée" (which is old) and "Bonne journée" (which is rather new). These changes are occurring simultaneously in many languages, but independently of one another it seems to me. They are not Anglicisms.

Another sign of the times is the scrupulousness, even nervousness, that our society exhibits in the observance of certain rites whose origin is very remote from us in time but whose importance, in the form they assume today, becomes greater with each passing year. One of the most characteristic of these rites is *gift-giving*. Like all rites, of course, it aims at strengthening social ties while helping to promote commerce. It is often said that this rite is manipulated by big business in the interest of increasing consumption. This is true, of course, but it is not the whole truth. The proof that gift-giving is a true rite is that it is governed by strict rules. Observing them requires extraordinary adroitness, because ultimately, in seeking to reconcile the imperative of reciprocity and equality with the no less essential imperative of difference, they contradict one another.

The structure of gift-giving as Mauss described it—giving-receiving-giving back—is still found in its contemporary manifestations. If one of the two gifts is more expensive than the other, the disfavored recipient does not dare to show his disappointment, but he is embittered just the same. Nor is the more favored recipient pleased, for he cannot help but wonder whether the superiority of the gift he received is indirectly a criticism of the gift he gave. He feels suspected of stinginess.

If the difference between the gifts reflects a sizeable inequality in the wealth of the two parties to the transaction, the result will be even worse. Far from being satisfied, the more favored recipient will be filled with resentment. He will have the impression that his wealthier counterpart wishes to humiliate him.

Prudence requires a no less strict equivalence in the giving of gifts than in the bartering of goods. Each party must imitate the other as closely as possible, while at the same time giving an impression of spontaneity. Each must convince the other that, in selecting the gift he gives him, he has obeyed an irresistible impulse, a sudden inspiration uncontaminated by the petty-minded calculations of ordinary people.

Imagine you were to make me a gift of a magnificent pen. How will you react if, immediately afterwards, I solemnly present you with a beautifully wrapped box, done up with ribbons and containing exactly the same pen—same manufacturer, same model, same color? You will feel horribly offended.

Let us now suppose that I present you with this same pen, only not right away and not the same color. My gift remains unacceptable. Suppose, then, I compensate for this insufficient difference by giving you a pen made by a different manufacturer, with a different nib, a very special type of ink, and so on. That ought to be enough to put matters right, it would appear, but just when my gift seems to be sufficiently different from yours, a new peril arises, namely, that you may suspect that the extraordinary pen I have given you is a subtle criticism of the more ordinary pen that you gave me.

In the world today, as in all the worlds of the past, one escapes the Charybdis of insufficient difference only in order to fall into the Scylla of excessive difference. It would not be surprising to learn that there are more attacks of depression every year when the season of gift-giving arrives. The sad thing is that, far from being imaginary, the anxiety aroused by gift-giving is justified. As all sacrificers knew in ancient times, the more a rite is to be trusted when it succeeds, the more it is to be dreaded when it fails. If rules, even the most Byzantine rules, are not all respected, gift-giving as a source of peace and harmony is diabolically transformed into a reason for infinite annoyance and irritation.

The anxiety aroused by gift-giving allows us to appreciate the wisdom of the natives of the Trobriand Islands of Papua New Guinea, who sustained and perpetuated neighborly relations by constantly exchanging not ephemeral and consumable gifts, but sacred objects—and always the same ones. The inhabitants of one island would solemnly convey them by canoe to their neighbors, who kept them for a certain time before passing them on again, just as solemnly, to the inhabitants of another neighboring island, and so on. Thanks to the perpetual rotation of these objects, everyone offered and received gifts that were equivalent, because they were always the same; and yet always unexpected and mysterious, because they were sacred. Bronislaw Malinowski described this system of exchange in his masterpiece, *Argonauts of the Western Pacific*.[2] It did not require the very considerable expenditure of money, energy, time, and thought that our system demands; nor could it arouse poisonous comparisons. It had all the advantages of modern gift-giving and none of the disadvantages.

By small successive degrees, then, our relations with one another can be degraded without anyone ever having to feel responsible for degrading them. The violence of non-violent persons (as we all believe ourselves to be) is never the work of particularly aggressive individuals whom appropriate prophylactic measures—ritual expulsion, for example—would keep from harming us. Nor is it the product of an aggressive instinct, an indelible trait of human nature to which we must adapt. It is the result of a negative collaboration that our narcissistic blindness prevents us from detecting.

To escape responsibility for violence we imagine it is enough to pledge never to be the first to do violence. But no one ever sees himself as casting the first stone. Even the most violent persons believe that they are always reacting to a violence committed in the first instance by someone else.

Moralists advise us all to avoid violence, of course, but only insofar as this is possible. They authorize us, at least tacitly, to reply to obvious provocations by the measured counterviolence that I described earlier, and which seems to us always justified. They do not seriously inquire into the legitimacy of their own claim to be exercising a legitimate right of self-defense.[3] This blindness to mimeticism opens the way to fresh outbreaks of self-aggravating violence. It should comes as no surprise that our moralists have not succeeded in altering the familiar dynamics of violence in any way. They share the habitual illusions on this subject—which is precisely why their teaching pleases us. They reassure us of our innocence and encourage us in our pious regret of the widening scope of violence, without ever awakening in us the least doubt with regard to ourselves, without ever suggesting that we ourselves, each of us in our own small way, might contribute to the very universality we deplore in this regard.

If the dynamism of even the most insignificant conflicts is as insidious as I suspect, violence is in us as well as around us. The only texts that fully recognize the mimetic character of human relations are the Gospels. The relevant injunctions are spoken in the famous Sermon on the Mount (Matthew 5:38–40):

> "You have heard that it was said, 'An eye for an eye and a tooth for a tooth.' But I say to you, offer no resistance to one who is evil. When someone strikes you on [your] right cheek, turn the other one to him as well. If anyone wants to go to law with you over your tunic, hand him your cloak as well."

Most people today regard these injunctions as a utopian sort of pacifism, manifestly naïve and even blameworthy because servile, doloristic, perhaps even masochistic. This interpretation betrays the influence of an ideology that sees veiled political agendas everywhere and attributes what it considers to be the irrationality of human behavior to mere superstition.

Is Jesus really asking us to grovel at the feet of just anybody, to beg for a slap in the face that no one dreams of giving us, to seek to satisfy the whims of the powerful at all costs? This reading pays only glancing attention to Saint Matthew's text, which presents us with two examples: someone who slaps us without provocation; and someone who sues us for our tunic, the main article of clothing, often the only one, in Jesus's world. Gratuitously reprehensible conduct of this sort suggests the presence of an ulterior motive. We are dealing with people who wish to infuriate us, to draw us into a cycle of escalating conflict. They do everything they can, in other words, to provoke a response that will justify them in retaliating in turn; to manufacture an excuse for legitimate self-defense. For if we treat them as they treat us, they will be able to disguise their own injustice by means of reprisals that are fully warranted by the violence we have committed. It is therefore necessary to deprive them of the negative collaboration that they demand of us.

Violent persons must always be disobeyed, not only because they encourage us to do harm, but because it is only through disobedience that a lethally contagious form of collective behavior can be short-circuited. Only the conduct enjoined by Jesus can keep violence from getting out of hand, by putting a stop to it before it starts. The object of a lawsuit, precious though it may be, is generally limited, finite, insignificant by comparison with the infinite risk that accompanies the least concession to the spirit of retaliation, which is to say to another round of mimeticism. It is better to hand over the tunic.

In order to properly understand the passage in Matthew, we need to recall the one in Saint Paul's letter to the Romans (12:20) in which Paul says that to renounce retaliation is to heap "burning coals" upon the heads of one's enemy; in other words, to place him in a morally impossible position. At first sight this sort of tactical advice seems quite unlike Jesus. It seems to suggest the practical effectiveness of non-violence, with a dash of cynicism. But this impression is more apparent than real. To speak of cynicism here is to minimize what non-violence actually requires us to do the moment violence is unleashed against us.

My own remarks here and in the pages that follow can be fully understood only in the context of the world in which we live, henceforth constantly under the threat of our own violence. Even if it used to be possible to regard the Sermon on the Mount as somehow unrealistic, this is no longer an option. Faced with our ever-growing powers of destruction, naiveté has changed sides. All human beings now have the same vital interest in preserving peace. In a truly global world, the renunciation of violent reprisal is bound to become, in a more and more obvious way, the indispensable condition of our survival.

CHAPTER 2

Noble Savages and Others

T he first ethnological investigations of primitive religions naturally attracted the interest of scientific journalists and popularizers since they combined ritual cannibalism and human sacrifice with other exotic forms of violence of which the public was fond. The moral superiority of the West seemed as obvious then to Westerners as its technological superiority, and encouraged a sensationalism that persists today only in third-rate publications. The popular hunger for violence is as great as ever, but the media now look for examples elsewhere than in archaic religion for fear of offending public opinion, which today is more respectful of non-Western cultures than it once was.

The horrors of the last war and the end of the colonial empires have forced Westerners to reflect upon their own violence. This is real progress. One can only hope that our knowledge of religion will one day be its beneficiary. For the moment, alas, research in the anthropology of religion is at a standstill. The great dispute between the West and archaic cultures is now refereed by politics and fashion, whose excesses have reached the point that anything which threatens to tarnish the good reputation of these cultures is condemned. The anachronistic perspective of political correctness is so influential today, in fact, that some reputable museums of Amerindian ethnology in the United States minimize violence, or even ignore it altogether, in presenting the history of religion and war in native American societies.

To justify this condemnation it has become necessary to reject all testimony that contradicts it, and in particular ethnological studies carried out prior to the disappearance of archaic religions, which by now is virtually complete. This ostracism is justified in its turn by the claim that all research prior to the present era of multiculturalism was the product and instrument of Western imperialism.

Nonsense. Most of the early ethnologists were deeply sympathetic to the cultures they studied. Even so, they made no attempt to hide the fact that many of the customs of these cultures are shocking to modern sensibilities. And even if, as a rule, the early ethnologists looked benevolently upon the archaic world, there were exceptions, not all of them negligible by any means. The celebrated *Golden Bough*, for example, the only classic of ethnology still read today, scarcely conceals its contempt for the detestable "superstitions" of the "primitive savages" to whom its author, Sir James G. Frazer, nonetheless did the honor of dedicating his monumental work.

On closer examination it is plain that Frazer and his followers, who, seen from a distance, seem to conform to the image that our age has formed of them, were in fact rather different. The ideology in which they were steeped was not the elementary racism that our age sees everywhere, but the religion of progress, then ascendant, whose tacit appeal to the faithful to take part in combatting Christianity was very warmly received in Frazer's time. If the early ethnologists took a rather severe line toward archaic religions, it was in order to condemn by implication a newer faith, which, like many of our own contemporaries, they interpreted as a myth of death and resurrection similar to the one they found in every religion that came before it, and which they believed to have been unduly privileged by Western ethnocentrism.

There can be no doubt that these ethnologists considered the West to be superior to other cultures. But it was superior only in the sense that it had gotten a head start on the road leading to skepticism about religion. Their Occidentalism, in other words, was more historicist than racist. No doubt the West was not yet as skeptical as it needed to be in their eyes. But it was nonetheless nearer to the ideal than other parts of the world, and could be counted on to reach it first—thanks in large part to the work of ethnologists.

This ethnology reflects the strengths as well as the weaknesses of the philosophy then dominant in academic circles, a positivism that, notwithstanding its obvious limitations, must still today be commended for its emphasis on patient observation and careful description. Anyone who grows tired of glorifying archaic cultures in the abstract cannot help but wish to get to know them, if not at first hand, then at least at second hand. It will be with gratitude and admiration that he discovers the quite extraordinary encyclopedia of information about such cultures compiled by the ethnologists of the late nineteenth and early twentieth centuries.

Every bit as much as the accounts of Herodotus and Thucydides, written for a certain Greek audience, the work of these authors, especially the British ethnologists, is our sole source of knowledge today of whole worlds that, but for them, would have vanished without a trace. The scope and detail of their field research, as I discovered in preparing to write *Violence and the Sacred*, are unrivalled in the history of cultural transmission.

Far from making a clean break with the way in which Westerners conceived of the relation between their culture and other cultures, notably archaic ones, the anti-Western furor today, by a great irony, revives a way of thinking that is typically, and even exclusively, Western.

When an individual belonging to one culture comes into contact with a foreign culture, he can, quite obviously, react only in one of two opposite ways: either he prefers his own culture or he prefers the foreign culture. The most frequent, the most natural, and also the most cultured reaction is to prefer one's own culture. This reaction is dominant in every culture, without exception, Western cultures not excluded.

In archaic and traditional societies, more than in modern society, individuals owe everything to their own culture. They cannot distance themselves from it, at least not so far that they are able to criticize it. For most cultures, even today, self-criticism remains inconceivable.

Every culture takes a dim view of anyone who does not unconditionally prefer the native to the foreign, the inside to the outside, and who does not blindly obey religious imperatives. If it is true, as I suppose, that these imperatives arose in archaic cultures from an original expulsion that exploits this fundamental distinction between inside and outside, between the acceptable and the unacceptable, those who reject them are liable to be expelled in their turn. All the other members of the society will unite against them by reproducing the founding act of violence, the act that serves as a model for all sacrifices, for all religious rites of purification. The preference that cultures grant to themselves, in other words, must be perpetuated at any cost. This preference is inseparably bound up with the identity, the autonomy, the very existence of these cultures.

The Western world is unique in this respect as in many others. Alongside the tendency, common to all cultures, of individuals to share a set of attachments—to one's family, one's city, one's nation, the West as a whole—another tendency very quickly appeared in opposition to those very same attachments. This countertendency has always been a minority attitude, I think, but it succeeded in putting down roots and spreading, especially in our time, to the point that it appears normal and legitimate. Outside the West, I have the impression that cultural self-criticism does not exist, or else remains in an embryonic state.

Westerners, in short, invented a new way of thinking about the relation between their culture and foreign cultures, a dramatic departure from the simple self-adulation found in all cultures. It proceeds by selecting a foreign cultural system and then comparing a Western system to it with a view to demonstrating the superiority of the foreign system. The Western habit of self-adulation is resisted, in other words, by admiring, or pretending to admire, another culture. This is why archaic cultures have enjoyed a great vogue in the West during the past five hundred years among thinkers, writers, and artists, at times bordering on blind (although usually short-lived) infatuation.

This sort of cultural self-criticism is always secondary to the self-adulation it seeks to combat. But it is by no means new. One finds it already in the literature of the Renaissance, notably in Montaigne's famous essay "Of Cannibals," in which he describes his encounter with three Tupinambá Indians in Rouen. The Tupinambá were a people living along the Atlantic coast of northeastern Brazil whose religious system was founded on a practice of cannibalism that ritualized the mutual hatred of two neighboring tribes. The two tribes were constantly at war with each other. Each made a practice of taking prisoners. They were treated decently at first, encouraged to marry and have children, and accepted as members of the community. Like many other cultures, the Tupinambá believed that captives were fit for sacrifice only once they had been integrated into a community. At that point they were killed, then devoured in revenge against the rival group, which treated its prisoners in the same fashion. The same cannibalistic violence was repeated again and again on each side, and always with a single purpose: to avenge the acts of violence committed by the other group.

Montaigne mentions neither the name nor the place of origin of the Tupinambá. Their customs do not seem to have interested him. One wonders if he actually laid eyes on these men. They provided him with a pretext for uncharacteristically utopian flights of fancy and amusing satirical quips, of course, all of which were more readily appreciated if the reader knew nothing about the anthropological context. This may be why the publishers of Montaigne's *Essays* were careful to say as little as possible about the Tupinambá.

At the end Montaigne asks rhetorically why the French do not take the Indians seriously, and then answers his own question: "They don't wear breeches." Does Montaigne himself take his subject seriously? The few allusions he makes to cannibalism are hardly critical of the practice. Montaigne wished to make it clear, I think, that he mistrusted what was said about the Tupinambá. Already, more than four centuries ago, he suspected a perverse invention of Western ethnocentrism, much as today's multiculturalists are eager to do.

Skepticism always has a distinct advantage over belief in matters of intellectual debate. Unfortunately for Montaigne, we are very well informed about the Tupinambá through his own contemporaries, travellers captured by the Tupinambá who managed to escape. Their accounts are independent of one another and yet they agree in the main. Far from being hostile to the Indians, these witnesses are almost as politically correct as Montaigne. Their tales are lucid and precise.

The most impressive thing to my mind is the unmistakably sacrificial logic that characterizes these writings, although it is not explicitly mentioned since obviously the authors were unacquainted with it. This logic is common to a very sizeable part of the two Americas, and its chief elements can be identified only by comparing a great number of cultures with one another. The rites of the Tupinambá, for example, bear a marked similarity to certain Aztec rites without being exactly the same. The authors of the Brazilian accounts surely did not make them up.

One will never know whether Montaigne's equanimity regarding cannibalism is due to skepticism or indifference. In either case I am disappointed.
Better, it seems to me, from the anthropological point of view, is Alfred
Métraux's essay about the earliest accounts of the Tupinambá. Drawing on
a thesis he had submitted to the Sorbonne in 1928, and then published in
a revised version more than two decades later, in 1951, Métraux took issue
with the findings of the latest wave of primitivist research, which benefitted
from the extraordinary popular enthusiasm for the work of a brilliant young
ethnologist named Claude Lévi-Strauss. In his preface, Métraux remarks
ironically that "these Indians, who seem so fierce to us today, were nevertheless at the origin of the myth of the 'noble savage.'"[1]

After the Renaissance, the passion for self-criticism subsided and the opposite tendency regained the upper hand. In France, the return to the West soon
merged with the cult of the absolute monarchy, of which Louis XIV was at
once the object, priest, and leader of the faithful. Then, in the eighteenth
century, a new and still stronger wave of primitivism swept over Europe, leaving behind a number of literary masterpieces, among them Montesquieu's
Persian Letters and Swift's *Gulliver's Travels*, as well as Voltaire's *L'Ingenu*
and *Candide*—not omitting Rousseau's *Discourse on Inequality*, in which the
natural man appears as the supreme avatar of the noble savage.

The Enlightenment and its revolutionary climax were immediately succeeded by another return to the West, now entering an age of capitalist and
industrial expansion. An unprecedented mood of optimism reigned among
the conquering bourgeois of northern and northwestern Europe in the nineteenth century, the golden age of faith in the unlimited progress of a world
brought together and guided by the West. Mimetic rivalries among Western
nations excited the colonialist impulse to a feverish state of recklessness and
arrogance, calmed only by the disastrous outcome of the First World War.
A second global conflict soon delivered the fatal blow, setting in motion
the latest swing of the pendulum, the greatest primitivist wave of all, whose
effects are still felt today.

Multiculturalism, or pluralism, though it does not wish to acknowledge
its Western heritage, can be understood only on the basis of this oscillation
between two opposed perspectives that for centuries now has informed

Western thinking about culture in general. The intensity of contemporary feeling prevents scholars from recognizing what is, after all, a quintessentially Western phenomenon. And yet this very same intensity testifies to its reality. Today's multiculturalism is the culmination, though not necessarily the final episode, of the escalating dynamic that has characterized primitivism from the beginning, and that is strengthened with each swing of the pendulum in either direction. The alternation of primitivism and Occidentalism has long shown itself to be a source of great intellectual creativity. It is inseparable, quite obviously, from the astonishing power of assimilation and revitalization that has characterized the West for at least a thousand years.

One may nonetheless wonder whether the fecundity of this dynamic has not now at last been exhausted, and whether from now on it will produce anything more than sterile vituperation. In certain university departments of anthropology in the United States today, students are taught that the only qualified observer of a human culture is someone who has belonged to it from birth. This doctrine denies what made the spirit of the Renaissance and the Enlightenment great—the craving for universally communicable knowledge. Multiculturalism frequently succumbs to the very thing that it denounces as the chief sin of the West, a longing for splendid isolation. Rather than work toward greater openness and mutual understanding, it shuts itself up within a world of artificially reconstituted non-Western cultures.

It is in our nature as human beings that we escape one excess only to fall into its contrary. With each swing of the pendulum, the transition becomes more abrupt, but also more abstract. The extremist rhetoric of the present day may well be the sign of an impoverishment of content, a loss of substance. In passing from one extreme to the other we do no more than convert positive into negative signs, a seesaw effect whose significance grows smaller by the day. We now resemble insomniacs who cannot sleep on either their right or their left side, and constantly toss and turn without finding any rest.

If one looks more closely at the pattern of alternation between the two currents, the question arises whether their increasingly theatrical contrast is not meant to conceal just the opposite, their similarity to each other. Self-criticism, even in its most brilliant periods, has always been a minority taste. But at certain times, such as the present day, it acquires a prestige that causes its influence to become preponderant. In the past this produced real transformations, notwithstanding the somewhat doubtful and vague quality first noticed in Montaigne's essay on cannibals. The primitivism descended from the myth of the noble savage is immune to criticism today in the West, where it has become an article of faith. It is now unarguably the central doctrine of mainstream anthropology.

One result of this is that primitivism has lost all its subversive force. And what is true of primitivism is true also of the Occidentalism that grew up in opposition to it, and that no longer bears any relation to the traditionalism of archaic cultures. With every swing of the pendulum, Western self-adulation incorporates the effects of the primitivist interregnum, and particularly its essential principle, cultural self-criticism, which increasingly is perceived as something specifically Western. The superiority of the West, in other words, is no longer founded on permanence, but rather on change.

Far from signifying the turning inward upon itself of an unchanging and unchangeable culture, Occidentalism exalts the Western power of revitalization. But this power rests on primitivism, no less than the scientific spirit itself and the glorification of the West's astounding technological prowess. Western self-criticism and self-adulation are therefore linked with each other in a paradoxical and self-reinforcing convergence whose reality no one dares acknowledge. These twin traditions call to mind those mimetic doubles whose mutual hostility is compounded once they discover how alike they really are. They do everything possible to conceal their resemblance, constantly detecting differences where there are none. Though they are antagonists, they need each other in order to perpetuate the discord that is their lifeblood. The secret understanding of these doubles, their complicity, is aimed at preventing the disclosure of a truth they conspire to cover up—a truth that, were it to be revealed, they fear would destroy them both.

To dispose of the empty opposition between self-criticism and self-adulation that still today concentrates everyone's attention, one must understand what it hides from view. The outstanding feature of the Occidentalism of someone like Frazer is the effort to exonerate the West of its own violence by throwing it back onto archaic and traditional cultures, which find themselves accused of obscurantism. In the classroom of progress there are bright students and there are dim students. The dim ones, if they are not dealt with firmly, threaten to hold back the entire class. They are the ones who are responsible for disorder and discord in a world that seeks constantly to move forward.

All this is perfectly ludicrous, of course, and contemporary primitivism is right to denounce it. The true threat to the world today comes from the mad ambitions of states and capitalists bent on destroying non-modern cultures. It is the so-called developed countries that plunder the planet's resources without showing the least concern for consequences they are incapable of foreseeing.

When archaic societies are demeaned in order to make the West look more honorable, what is really going on? One is dividing humanity in two and sealing them off from each other, the archaic world on the one side, the modern world on the other—with violence being reserved for archaic and traditional cultures alone. That is exactly what Frazer did. Those who do the opposite, who idealize archaic societies in order to denigrate the West, see themselves as very different, but in the last analysis they do precisely the same thing. They too divide the world into two compartments that they imagine to be completely isolated from each other, and then put violence in one of them, this time the modern compartment.

But isn't this view truer than the other one, its proponents will object? Relocating violence in an archaic world that no longer poses a threat to anyone, since by now it is quite dead, only makes a mockery of the modern world. The falsity of that view was already plain in Frazer's time; now, they maintain, it is simply grotesque. Moreover, it is just the position that I uphold in forever insisting on the violence of archaic religions. In so doing, don't I prove that I, too, am a lackey of Western imperialism?

Archaic violence is insignificant, to be sure, in any absolute sense. This would be a relevant point if I were concerned to establish our shared responsibility for the dangers that confront the world today and the injustices that dishonor it. But there is no shortage of people who will undertake to right wrongs and defend the cause of justice. I therefore concern myself with something else. I am interested in archaic violence for reasons that are quite different from Frazer's. My purpose is not to draw up an indictment of archaic societies.

Those who suppose that I am hostile to these societies do not understand the point of my work. The importance of primitive violence has to do with its symbolic clarity. To explain our own violence we must compare it with ritual sacrifices and look for resemblances between them. Mimetic anthropology, unlike its competitors, does not shy away from doing this. I do not pretend, of course, that the violence of primitive societies is at all commensurate with modern violence. Its absolute power is nil, and its ecological consequences for the most part are no greater. And yet it is not, for all that, negligible.

Frazer remains significant because he discovered that scapegoats in the ritual sense are encountered everywhere in archaic cultures, and not only in the book of Leviticus. He enlarged the meaning of an expression that deserves to be enlarged, first in the way that Frazer did, and then in a second and still more significant way. Lévi-Strauss thinks that my use of the term "scapegoat" is proof of the risible amateurishness of my work. The very term annoys him. It has no importance in and of itself; the Greek word *phármakos*, or indeed any other term designating the victim of a ritual expulsion, would do just as well—but only so long, of course, as its meaning is extended beyond what Frazer meant by it, beyond its ritual significance, in order to capture the psychosocial phenomenon that is hidden by the rite itself and that stands fully revealed in our time because it is no longer ritualized.

That is what Frazer was incapable of doing. He never understood that, behind the ritual scapegoat, there is something more than mere superstition; there is also the tendency, universal among human beings, to take out their anger on a substitute, on an alternative victim. We now detect this strange phenomenon without the least difficulty because rites are no longer there to conceal it from us.

Neither Frazer nor Lévi-Strauss doubted that scapegoats still exist, typically in attenuated form, but in any case a form that is fundamentally identical to the one they have in archaic religion. Everywhere and always, when human beings either cannot or dare not take their anger out on the thing that has caused it, they unconsciously search for substitutes, and more often than not they find them. This was true of the "primitive savages" stigmatized by Frazer, and it was true of the subjects of Her Majesty, Queen Victoria—and true also, then, for James George Frazer himself. It is this that he could not imagine.

The universal reality of the scapegoat phenomenon from which Frazer shrank has long found expression in all Western languages, without anyone ever having noticed. It is made manifest each time someone gives the word "scapegoat," in daily life, the psychosocial meaning that anthropology stubbornly refuses to acknowledge, the sense that we all understand when we say that such and such a person is being used as a scapegoat by his family, his colleagues, the media, and so forth.

Multiculturalists today have managed to see what Frazer missed, however, and on this point at least one must give them their due. They are not mistaken about the world in which we live: it is indeed full of more or less hidden victims. Alas, our young iconoclasts have purchased this clearsightedness at the cost of a blindness that is the opposite of Frazer's. They fail to see that in the archaic world there was the same type of victim, the same scapegoat. Everything Frazer and his followers did not see the multiculturalists see, but everything Frazer and his followers did see they no longer see. Each of the two schools lucidly detects the half of the truth that its adversary ignores, the better to make itself blind to the other half.

The most recent phase of the alternation between Occidentalism and primitivism has therefore concealed the essential thing, the universality of violence. A selective blindness in one of two forms has obscured the fact that all cultures, and all individuals without exception, participate in violence; that violence is what structures our collective sense of belonging and our personal identities.

Faced with a phenomenon as vast, as variable, as diverse, and nonetheless as repetitive as religion, one cannot help but search for an invariant form of which its innumerable manifestations are so many more or less similar instances.

Religion, it will be said, has no such invariant. There is none in the strict sense, that I admit. But there is a quasi-invariant that has yet to be systematically investigated, even though it has proven historically to be prodigious in its consequences, namely, the violence internal to human communities. Reconceiving anthropology in the light of this violence, which is to say making it a new point of departure for the study of religion, is what I have been attempting to do.

There is no human society that is not liable to break down as a result of its own violence. Every society seeks to thwart this tendency through a specific behavior of which it resolutely remains unaware, and which anthropology has never discovered. I have in mind, of course, the spontaneous, mimetic convergence of an entire community upon a single victim—the descendant of an original scapegoat—on whose head all hatreds are discharged so that they will not spread with catastrophic effect, destroying the community.

When *Violence and the Sacred* came out, some readers suspected me of having a morbid taste for violence. Today I am supposed to be passionately devoted to the cause of non-violence. This is more agreeable, to be sure, but it is no less false. What got me interested in violence in the first place was the hope of succeeding where the old anthropology had failed—in giving a systematic explanation of myths and rites. This enterprise would be impossible, I think, if we did not have access to another source of illumination, an unexpected one, as it happens, since it involves a relatively modern set of religious texts, the Bible and the four accounts of the Passion. These texts illuminate the process of manufacturing victims from within by exposing the error of the charge brought against scapegoats before and after Christ, all of whom were wrongly accused and condemned. Once the morphogenetic power of this error is grasped it becomes possible to decipher all mythical and sacrificial forms.

If the indictment of Jesus had been entirely successful, if this scapegoat had, like all the others, been unanimously vilified, the Gospels really would be just another myth. But the attempt to victimize Jesus manifestly failed. The four gospel accounts are the record of this failure. Thus it is that the Cross of Christ came to have the universal power of revelation proclaimed by Saint Paul.

CHAPTER 3

Mimetic Theory
and Theology

Raymund Schwager attributes an essential role in Christian redemption to the phenomenon of the scapegoat.[1] What does this phenomenon involve? The Gospels tell us. They portray Jesus as a victim, sentenced to death *for no reason*, in the wake of a wave of contagious violence that furnished those who were caught up in it with false reasons, false grounds for accusation. We are not dealing here with the animal of Leviticus, the ritual victim designated in that book by the term "scapegoat," but with the term's familiar modern meaning, someone unjustly condemned by a group of people who have been mimetically mobilized against him.

Jesus himself announced that his death would resemble that of the Servant of the Lord in Second Isaiah and other prophets who were collectively assassinated or mistreated under circumstances similar to those of the Passion. In saying that God made Jesus the bearer of all our sins, the sinner par excellence, Paul says the same thing in different terms. From all these textual convergences, Schwager draws the inescapable conclusion:

> In the usual operation of the scapegoat mechanism, the transfer takes place only partially. Ultimately, therefore, violence is never totally diverted to the outside; it can always break out anew. Yet all the Gospels show that

Jesus's message of God's unfathomable love and his own claim to be
completely one with God brought to light the most deep-seated resentment and the secret will to kill even in the pious and educated Pharisees.
... [T]he scapegoat mechanism is superbly suited to help bring one to a
deeper understanding of the New Testament statement that Jesus as the
holy one was made into a sin and a curse. This opens the way for a more
penetrating understanding of the doctrine of redemption.[2]

Among my own works, the one that corresponds most closely to Schwager's book *Must There Be Scapegoats?* is a conversation with Jean-Michel
Oughourlian and Guy Lefort published under the title *Things Hidden Since
the Foundation of the World*.[3] On most of the topics that are common to the
two, both works, without always using exactly the same language or the same
examples, expound the same doctrine—with one exception, which the para-
graph I have just quoted summarizes. I saw the logic of Schwager's argument,
but I could not bring myself to approve it. It aroused in me a feeling of unease
that over time grew fainter and finally disappeared.

Schwager's intuition now seems to me correct. To pay tribute to him, I
will try to answer the question that my reluctance to share his opinion poses
in retrospect. What was it that prevented me from seeing Jesus as a scapegoat
who sacrificed himself for mankind? What was it that stopped me from taking the step that Schwager took at once?

While Schwager's thinking is unambiguously situated in a theological frame-
work, mine approaches the Judeo-Christian tradition from the perspective
of modern anthropology. My thinking remains bound up with anthropology, if only negatively, for I see mimetic theory first and foremost as a means
of subverting the intellectual foundations of the relativism that dominates
our world.

In the ancient world the defenders of paganism denied the singular
character of Christianity on the basis of *resemblances* between the sequence
of events described in the Gospels and many mythical sequences. A number
of pagan gods and demigods (Dionysus, Osiris, and Adonis, for example)
experienced an agonizing ordeal, a moment of tortured inspiration that calls
to mind the Passion. The violence to which they were subjected emerges in

the frenzy of social disorder, or absence of order; and it is followed by a kind of resurrection, a triumphant reappearance of the victim, who reestablishes order and thus reveals his divinity.

Ethnologists in the nineteenth and the early twentieth century found the same sequence of events more or less everywhere in archaic cults and related social institutions, such as sacred monarchies. Fascinated by these discoveries, they set out to elaborate a general theory of religion. This ambition was never successfully realized, and today it is considered to be unrealizable, indeed almost reprehensible. It is seen to be the result of a scholarly form of imperialism that is inevitably linked with a political form, namely, colonialism.

The charge is unwarranted. Many ethnologists were anticolonialists, and this at a time when opposing colonialism required considerably more courage than it does today. They were motivated by the same passion, at once scientific and antireligious, that inspired all the great intellectual adventures of the age, most notably Darwinism. They looked to find a universal essence of religion, in order to forever discredit the Christian claim to singularity. This meant demonstrating the similarities between religions. Today it is a question only of demonstrating the *differences* between them, but the change is more apparent than real. The diversity that is so noisily glorified today is insignificant, for it excludes the only difference that matters, the one that separates the true from the false, the real from the imaginary.

Religious relativism is a metaphysical certainty like any other. How can there be certainty once one no longer believes anything, at least not in principle—not even the demonstrations of science? Insist on having an answer to this question and you will end up having the similarities between myths and Christianity pointed out to you. They are too numerous and too striking, you will be told, for us not to rule out the possibility that Christianity is truly unique. Erase the differences, in other words, and you slide back all the way down to the rock bottom of religious relativism, the similarities I have just mentioned. Without knowing what these similarities signify, you are asked to take it for granted that they trump differences.

How does Judeo-Christian scripture fundamentally differ from Greco-Roman myth? Nietzsche answered this question very nicely. In biblical texts, victims are innocent and collective violence is to blame. In myths, the victims are to blame and communities are always innocent. Oedipus is truly guilty, truly responsible for the plague. The Thebans were therefore perfectly right to expel him. The Servant of the Lord and Jesus, on the other hand, are innocent. Their death is an injustice.

Nietzsche and the moderns who came after him see this as an essentially *moral* difference. In their view there is something contemptible about the word "moral." This contempt is most extreme in the case of Nietzsche himself, who unhesitatingly takes the side of myth against Judeo-Christian tradition. But if the Judeo-Christian defense of victims is indisputably more moral than the condemnation of victims in myths, it is not for the reason Nietzsche imagines, that taking the side of the victim is the sly, cunning revenge which the weak take upon the strong—what he calls "slave morality." It is more moral because it is the *truth*. Victims are scapegoats who have been selected solely through a process of violent mimeticism, which is why they are truly innocent. The coincidence of morality and truth in Judeo-Christian accounts completely escapes Nietzsche and his fellow moderns, for they do not grasp the role of unanimity in assuring that the victim will be a scapegoat.

Beneath the superficial similarities between myth and Judeo-Christian accounts, mimetic theory detects a series of actual events. The chaos that precedes collective violence is nothing other than this, the disintegration of human communities as a result of the mimetic rivalries that all human beings are liable to be caught up in. The contagion of mimeticism spreads as it becomes more acute, and winds up reintegrating what earlier it had disintegrated. It reunifies communities against scapegoats, which is to say victims who are wrongly considered to be responsible for disorders that come about through a process of mimetic contagion alone.

Only mimetic theory can explain why the victims in myths seem to be guilty and the communities innocent. This impression is due to an illusion aroused by the spread of violence. Myths are rooted in crowd phenomena, which fool both the makers of myths and their audience. Myths are incapable of critically examining even the most implausible accusations that one encounters more or less everywhere in them, so-called Oedipal crimes such as parricide, incest, bestiality, the transmission of disease, and so on. The "sins" of mythical heroes are too reminiscent of the ones associated with bloodthirsty crowds not to be the product of the same mentality.

If myths fool us by standing the true relation between victims and communities on its head, Judeo-Christian texts reestablish, or perhaps establish for the first time, a truth that in every case is detected by reversing the original reversal. They get right what is always the wrong way around in myths, namely, the relation between isolated, powerless victims and the communities that persecute them. Judeo-Christian texts, in other words, reveal what myths conceal. The defense of victims is therefore not merely a piece of sermonizing. In proclaiming the truth of scapegoats, the Judeo-Christian perspective undermines the whole mythical system, for the lie it denounces plays an essential role in human culture. Some myths do, of course, downplay the guilt of victims; but not one of them incriminates the persecuting community.

Why do myths and biblical narratives resemble each other as much as they do? Because they are all confronted by the same type of crisis, the same machine for manufacturing false victims. Why do biblical narratives differ from myths more than they resemble them? Because they respond to this trial differently than myths do.

In the case of myths, the machine for manufacturing false victims functions so efficiently, so irresistibly, that all opposition is eliminated. It is this result that myths treat as though it were something true and necessary. In the case of biblical narratives, the machine still functions, only less and less well, so that finally, in both the Old and the New Testaments, it functions so badly that the entire truth of scapegoats and of the mechanism that produces them is unmasked.

The superiority of the Bible cannot be defined in terms of race, people, or nation; it is not at all ethnocentric. Jewish and Christian communities were no more successful than other communities, on the whole, in resisting contagious violence. Only small minorities resisted. Instead of being unanimous, as in myths, the hostility toward victims in biblical narratives involved only a majority of the community. Yet if submission to mimetic violence had not continued to prevail over resistance, and by a great margin, there would have been no scapegoat to rehabilitate.

Revelation was therefore uncommon for two reasons. Not only was it the product of a unique tradition, it operated only within recalcitrant minorities—within *remnants* that, although they were not powerful enough to overcome majority opinion, were nonetheless influential enough to guide the compilation of the holy scriptures and shape the great traditions of Judaism and Christianity. This is why, unlike in myths, where the dramatic resolution is invariably harmonious and "constructive," since it reflects the cathartic, purgative effect of violent unanimity, collective violence in Judeo-Christian texts produces disunion, especially emphasized in the Gospels. The synoptic Gospels all quote Jesus as saying that he brought war and not peace; John shows that Jesus provoked dissension and conflict wherever he went. The sudden intrusion of the truth destroyed a social harmony that depended on the lie of unanimous violence.

Mimetic theory makes it clear that the Judeo-Christian narratives do not recount myths. Each time the Bible describes collective violence, the tale it tells resembles a myth, but it is plainly distinguished from myth by the interpretation it contains. Myths are the passive reflection, and Judeo-Christian accounts the active reflection, of the same collective machine for manufacturing scapegoats: the violent, mimetic crowd.

Not only do Judeo-Christian accounts possess a truth that eludes all myths, they alone are aware of possessing it. It is not ethnocentric denial or rivalry with other religions that leads biblical tradition to claim a monopoly on this truth. Nietzsche was right about this one thing at least: no religion defends victims as vigorously as the Judeo-Christian heritage does. Nietzsche saw this as a sign of inferiority, of course, but we see it as a sign of superiority, one that refutes religious relativism on its own purely anthropological terms. It is impossible to imagine that, in the religion of the Incarnation, this superiority could be independent of the religious dimension.

The similarities between myths and Judeo-Christian narratives are as real as the early ethnologists had hoped, but their consequences are not the ones their anti-Christian bias led them to expect. If biblical texts resembled myths less than they do, they could not differ from myths as much as they do. The biblical texts would in that case be free from a fundamental human temptation, the same one that Peter experienced in the courtyard of the high priest—the pressure of social conformism. In that case they could not prevail over myths, as in fact they do, in the trial that both of them are made to undergo.

The early ethnologists were not wrong to try to systematize religion. But their hostility to Christianity concealed its meaning and purpose from them. They sought to reduce the Judeo-Christian tradition to the status of a myth. They sought to explain light by darkness, and, as one might expect, they wound up obscuring the truth. To illuminate it one must go about things

the opposite way, and read myths on the basis of the Judeo-Christian understanding of how victims are created.

Once the role of scapegoats in myths has been recognized, a rational explanation of archaic religion is readily deduced. A community tested by a long
crisis sees in its sudden deliverance a miracle for which it does not feel able
to take credit itself. It therefore looks for a scapegoat. This extraordinary
person, having spread disorder and death while alive, revives the community
in death. For better or for worse, his powers appear to transcend all human
finiteness. The archaic gods are sacralized scapegoats. In revealing their innocence, the Judeo-Christian tradition desacralizes scapegoats and brings the
age of myth to a close. Nothing is more striking, by way of contrast with
mythic accounts, than the humanity of a Joseph, of a Job, of the prophets,
and of all the rehabilitated victims with whom the Bible is filled.

Seen in the light of this desacralization, Christianity is unavoidably
problematic. For a Christian, Jesus's salvific power operates through the Passion, which is to say by means of a scapegoat phenomenon. But isn't this a
step backward then? Wasn't Christ himself a sacralized scapegoat as well?
Ultimately, when Christianity is compared unfavorably to the strict mono-
theisms of Judaism and Islam, it is just this perceived regression for which it
is being reproached. The force of such a criticism, and my desire to respond
to it, only deepened the hesitation I felt in the face of the argument made
by Schwager, which I quoted at the beginning of this chapter. For mimetic
theory, pushed to its logical conclusion, leaves us with a phenomenon that
is too similar to the archaic sacred not to encourage what mimetic theory in
other respects discourages, namely, the likening of Christianity to a myth.

The analysis I have just sketched shows that the divinity of Christ cannot be reduced to the sacralization of a scapegoat, however. This process
requires, as I say, that scapegoats be truly guilty. If their innocence were to
be recognized, they could no longer polarize violence, for they would have
lost their power to unite the community against them. If Christ had in fact
been divinized as the result of a violent act of sacralization, then the witnesses to the Resurrection would have been a mob howling for him to be
put to death, and not the few individuals who proclaimed his innocence. In
that case the peace of Christ would have been a peace made by the world, the

peace of scapegoats, and not the peace that "surpasses all understanding."[4] The kingdom of God, in other words, is not of this world. On earth, the Gospels promise only the division and discord that the collapse of violent unanimity makes inevitable.

If Christianity were to relapse into myth on a point as central as the divinity of Christ, this weakness would rapidly spread and give the New Testament as a whole a retrograde character by comparison with the Hebrew Bible. But, in fact, the New Testament completes the process of desacralization by revealing what is revealed nowhere else—the mimetic genesis of scapegoats, and their founding and organizing role in human culture. On a worldly level, the Passion is only one example among many of the scapegoat mechanism and its dominant influence in societies everywhere. But of all the accounts found in the Bible, it is the most completely demythologized example, the one that promises to teach us the most about the origin and operation in human societies of what the Gospels call earthly powers.[5]

The endlessly renewed effects of this process are indistinguishable from the long line of murders that goes back to the foundation of the world and that Jesus prolonged up until the moment of his own Passion. This theme of the synoptic Gospels must be compared with the claim in the Gospel According to John that the devil was "a murderer from the beginning."[6] If Satan is a principle of both order and disorder, it is because the mimetic violence for which his name is a synonym resolves itself in the mechanism of the scapegoat. This is also why he is taken in by the Cross, which deprived him of his chief resource. Satan understands too late that the pathetic secret of his power has been revealed and neutralized by the truthful accounts of the Passion, that is, by the Spirit of God, which imbues Jesus's disciples with the courage to proclaim the truth. This Spirit, it will be recalled, is called *Paraclete*, a word that means "advocate,"[7] a defender of victims.

Schwager understands all this. I understood it, too, at the time I was writing *Things Hidden Since the Foundation of the World*, but it did not satisfy me. The principal interest of mimetic theory to my mind is its apologetic power to combat religious relativism, whose weakness it unmasks. I wanted something still more explicit, a *sign*. What troubled me most of all, with regard to the Passion of Christ, was Schwager's reliance on the term "sacrifice," which I had used earlier in reference to the rituals of archaic religion. It seemed to me that the traditional definition of the Passion in terms of *sacrifice* furnished additional arguments to those who wished to liken Christianity to an archaic religion. This is why, for a long time, I resisted it.

What is a sacrifice in archaic religions? It is an effort to revive the conciliatory effects of unanimous violence by substituting an alternative victim for the original scapegoat. What is the sacrifice of Christ? This is harder to understand. One must begin at the beginning, which is to say with what Jesus proposed to men so that they might escape violence. He invited them to be done with mimetic rivalries. Each time a potential rival makes unreasonable demands of us, or what seem to us to be unreasonable demands, instead of treating him in the same manner one must yield on the issue in dispute; one must avoid escalating violence, which leads directly to scapegoating.

This is the sole rule of the Kingdom. And Jesus remained faithful to it until the end in a world that cared nothing about it. He found himself alone against all. The violence of men was turned against the one who called upon them to renounce it. His Word revealed more and more of the hidden truth of human culture, which is to say the founding and ordering role of scapegoats. The accomplishment of his mission therefore doomed Christ to a death that he scarcely desired, but one that he could not avoid without submitting to the law of the world, the law of scapegoats.

So great is the distance between the sacrifice of Christ in this sense and archaic sacrifice that a greater one cannot be imagined. To protect itself against its own violence, mankind had ended up directing it against innocents. Christ did just the opposite. He offered no resistance. It was not in order to play the game of his enemies that he gave himself up to be sacrificed, but in order to put an end to sacrifice, as we are now able to understand through mimetic theory. In making known to mankind the hold of sacrifice over it, as word of his death spread throughout the world, Christ loosened its grip, and so disabled at last a mechanism whose effectiveness depended on secrecy.

Mimetic theory illuminates the basic opposition between archaic sacrifice and what is customarily called the sacrifice of Christ. It is this opposition that the whole of modern culture manages not to see, stubbornly defining sacrifice in terms of a *gift* or *offering* to a divinity. This rather hypocritical willfulness makes it possible to constantly elide the question of violence, now comically reduced to an ingenious process deliberately invented to dispose of a gift, the victim, whom its givers cannot themselves hand over to a recipient, the divinity, who is forever absent.

To free ourselves from this sterile formalism we must adopt the point of view of biblical realism, particularly in relation to the judgment of Solomon. My thinking about sacrifice has been nourished from the beginning by this inexhaustible text.[8] Since allusions to the sacrifice of children are many in the Bible, I do not see why we should refrain from seeing one such reference in an account whose genius is made plain only by biblical realism.

To settle a dispute between two prostitutes over which one is the mother of a baby, Solomon orders it to be cut in two with the stroke of a sword and half of it to be given to each of them. In giving up the child to the other woman, the good prostitute puts an end to their mimetic rivalry, not through the method commanded by Solomon, bloody sacrifice, which the other woman has already accepted, but through love. She relinquishes her claim to the object of the rivalry. She does therefore what Christ would have urged her to do: she takes renunciation to its furthest possible extreme, for she renounces that which is dearest to a mother, her own child. Just as Christ died so that humanity might abandon the habit of violent sacrifice, the good prostitute sacrifices her own motherhood so that the child may live.[9]

What I found shocking was the failure to grasp the immensity of the chasm that separates the good prostitute from the bad one, the erasing of this difference by using the same term, sacrifice, in both cases. I therefore long reserved the term "sacrifice" for the solution imposed by Solomon, that is, for the type of sacrifice whose threat the selfless gesture of the good prostitute forever removes.

To justify this decision, I insisted on the prophetic criticism of sacrifice embraced by Jesus in the Gospels. I spoke of a non-sacrificial Christianity, which stands out as the only authentic faith among all the doctrines that have covered up and concealed human violence, among all the religions, philosophies, and other modes of thought that, implicitly or explicitly, are foreign to Christian revelation. In saying this much I was in no way trying to take issue with orthodox theological teaching, which in any case I knew little about. I wished only to dispel among non-Christians, and today among Christians themselves, the equivocation perpetuated by the ambivalence of the term "sacrifice." This concern still seems to me to be legitimate. But it must not be regarded as overriding or in any sense absolute. To clearly distinguish between two types of religion, the mythic and the Christian, I was searching for a symbolically manifest difference, something as visible and tangible as possible.

As it turns out I was mistaken, not once but twice. First, because the distinction I wished to make is not really indispensable, for the reasons I have just given. Second, because the use of the same word for both types of sacrifice, as misleading as it may be on one level, nevertheless suggests something essential, namely, the paradoxical unity of religion in all its forms throughout human history.

To recognize the positive sense of the term "sacrifice," when it encompasses the two extremes I have described, is not necessarily to minimize the distance between these two extremes, nor to amalgamate them by means of a bit of legerdemain involving the notion of a sacrificial offering. On the contrary, one must be fully aware of the unfathomable gulf between these two extremes. Mimetic theory aids us in this task. The further the extremes are from each other, the more their union in a single word paradoxically hints at a going beyond the opposition between them.

Solomon's judgment points to this going beyond, this forgoing of violence. The biblical account cannot be accused of minimizing the gulf between the two kinds of sacrifice. And yet in order to appreciate how much separates them, one cannot avoid comparing them. And indeed it is commonly said that the good prostitute *sacrificed* rivalry for the sake of her child, whereas the bad prostitute agreed to *sacrifice* the child for the sake of the rivalry.

What the biblical account says is that one can renounce sacrifice in one sense—sacrifice of another, violence against another—only by assuming the risk of sacrifice in another sense—the sacrifice of Christ, who died for all who were dear to him. Use of the same word in each case dispels the illusion of a neutral ground where violence is nowhere to be seen, and this from a non-sacrificial vantage point that sages and scholars can permanently occupy in order to apprehend the truth at minimal cost to themselves—perhaps even in order to Christianize the human sciences, as François Lagarde has dared to imagine.[10]

God Himself reuses the scapegoat mechanism, at his own expense, in order to subvert it. This tragedy is not devoid of irony. Indeed, its connotations are so rich that most of them escape us. The irony has to do in part with the structural similarity between the two kinds of sacrifice, which, at one extreme, exhibit odd mirror effects in relation to violence, and, at the other, a love that surpasses our understanding and our powers of expression.

The divine reuse of the scapegoat mechanism completed the religious unity of mankind. It may perhaps be thought of as a slow and terrible voyage from the first sort of sacrifice toward the second, accessible to us only through Christ. Between the violence of human origins and the schema of Christian redemption, one notices a symmetry that is not found in the intermediate stages of Judeo-Christian desacralization. From the symbolic point of view, in the perspective of these intermediate stages, one sees something like a return to archaic religion. This cannot help but seem puzzling. But it must not be interpreted as a falling back into the archaism of sacralized scapegoats. The resemblance is apparent instead because violence now imitates the love of Christ, and not the other way around. Not the least of the reasons why this should be so, as Ted Peters has suggested, is the fact that divine intervention is an exceedingly subtle phenomenon.[11] Without ever seeking to limit human freedom, and without ever allowing his revelation to become constraining or coercive, Christ guides humanity toward divine truth.

Christ is not simply another sacralized scapegoat. Christ became a scapegoat in order to desacralize those who came before him and to prevent those who come after him from being sacralized. It is as an interpreter of this role that he reveals himself both as the true god and as a man, long doomed to the colossal but inevitable error of holding God responsible for purely human violence. Christ, his Father, and the Paraclete are therefore themselves, the three of them, the one God who corresponds to John's definition—*God is love.*

It follows from this that there are two radically opposed yet formally similar modes of divinity: the archaic, which arises directly from the efficacy of scapegoats; and the Christian, which arises indirectly, and paradoxically, from their inefficacy by virtue of the destruction of false gods. As against the partial, earthly, temporal, and unjustly condemned scapegoats of all other religions, as Schwager observes, there is the perfect scapegoat, both fully human and fully divine. As against imperfect sacrifices, whose efficacy is temporary and limited, there is the perfect sacrifice that puts an end to all the others.

Some of the arguments I make in *Things Hidden Since the Foundation of the World* agree with what I have just said here, but others run contrary to it, particularly the critique of the Letter to the Hebrews, which now seems to me unfair. I now detect a hesitation, a flaw in my book that makes me appreciate Schwager's greater decisiveness.

PART 2

The Other Side of Myth

CHAPTER 4

I See Satan Fall
Like Lightning

MARIA STELLA BARBERI: In *I See Satan Fall Like Lightning* you propose a new reading of the Gospels, which you see as the source of mimetic theory.[1] Do you think that the debate to which the book gave rise has helped to clear up certain misunderstandings?

RENÉ GIRARD: To the Gospels one must add the Old Testament, for my book begins by considering the Tenth Commandment, which, basically, says that rivalrous mimetic desire is forbidden. Exodus and Deuteronomy already contained this prohibition, prior to the Gospels.

As for the book's reception, I don't want to go into the various criticisms that have been made in any great detail. It seems to me that the main point has been understood, namely, that the origins of mimetic theory are wholly to be found in biblical texts, old and new.

The moment I became aware that it issued from the Hebrew Bible and the Christian Gospels, I no longer felt able to claim authorship for myself, as I had done in *Deceit, Desire, and the Novel.*[2] In my next book, *Violence and the Sacred*, where I introduce mimetic theory in the sixth chapter, I still regarded it as my own invention.[3]

Starting out from the Bible, in order to show that it contains mimetic theory, as I have done in *I See Satan Falling Like Lightning*, nonetheless poses a compositional problem. The sequence of historical events is at odds with the order in which they came to be understood. It is difficult to accept the fact that the Gospels can help us to understand things that came before. There is a tendency instead to see the Gospels as an aid to understanding what, chronologically, came after.

Historical chronology should begin with the evolution of the human race, accompanied by the rising power of mimetic desire, which gave birth to crises of murderous and destructive violence for human populations. This violence is channeled through the designation and expulsion of scapegoats, a phenomenon of collective reconciliation that is at the root of all archaic cultures. Chronological order continues with Judaism and Christianity. The Gospels are therefore both what comes to an end, from a chronological point of view, and what comes at the beginning, in the order of understanding. In revealing that Christ's death was the death of an innocent victim, they reveal what preceded it: the mechanism by which a scapegoat is selected and expelled, and the mimetic dynamic that leads to this murder.

Probably I should have explained this at the outset of my last book. But to have done that would have been to take for granted the very thesis that I then go on to argue for. Everything proceeds from the Gospels and ends up with the Gospels. The problem, then, was to construct a chain of reasoning, beginning with the Gospels, that would show that an understanding of mimetic theory, which to my mind ought to come first, in fact comes from the Gospels.

There is no choice but to keep shuttling back and forth between alpha and omega. This constant movement, back and forth, imposes a form of composition resembling a snail, or a volute, or a spiral—a form that the reader is liable to find disconcerting, and in the worst case incomprehensible.

MSB: In other words, you understand why some readers didn't understand.

RG: I do. Most readers *have* understood, I hope, but the difficulty is convincing them of the scientific character of my approach. The word "scientific" does not apply here to the interpretation of the Gospels, but to the interpretation that the Gospels give of mythologies. The Gospels *read* myth. Once again, however, the attempt to show this runs up against chronological problems.

The reader expects things to be presented in historical order, and therefore expects me to begin with the archaic.

MSB: Still, the book's recurring theme is mimetic violence. You have to keep circling back to what came before in order to go forward, to make progress in explaining this phenomenon.

RG: That's right. The best way to approach the book, I think, is as a thriller. All of the pieces of the puzzle are given at the beginning, but it is only at the end that it becomes clear how they fit together.

MSB: The book begins with an analysis of scandal—*skándalon*, in the Greek—in order to arrive at Satan, and then moves from Satan to the triumph of the Cross. You begin, in other words, by examining the main elements on which the gospel reading of myth depends.

RG: Yes. For example, the Gospels explain why so many mythical heroes are frail, sick, or disabled. The Gospels explain not only the general structure of myths, but also other phenomena that modern scholars and scientists have never grasped. In Second Isaiah, it is said of the Servant of the Lord that "he had no majestic bearing to catch our eye, no beauty to draw us to him. He was spurned and avoided by men . . . [l]ike one from whom you turn your face . . ." (Isaiah 53:2–3). This passage describes the characteristic traits of scapegoats, and they apply quite readily to many mythical figures. In the so-called Servant Songs of the same book,[4] the prophet is frankly presented as a typical scapegoat, persecuted not only because he is a prophet, but because he's one of those whom no one—

MSB: Looks at.

RG: Precisely. What is more, these physical traits were associated by some Orthodox mystics with Christ himself. The Servant Songs in Second Isaiah, as well as similar passages in the Book of Job, are really immense psalms: they invert the mythic perspective, they turn the victim mechanism upside down in giving voice to the victim. In my last book, I use the metaphor of an animal hide that, instead of being worn with the smooth and lustrous fur on the outside, is turned inside out to display the bloody flesh of the victim.

MSB: You speak also of a glove turned inside out.

RG: Yes—this is what the great texts of the Old Testament do, they turn things inside out.

MSB: They discover a sort of *epistémè* of the victim.

RG: Nietzsche saw this clearly, since this *epistémè* is the very basis of the evangelical dissidence embodied by Christ's disciples. And yet he did not realize that what was at issue was truth. In mythic accounts, the opinion of the crowd is never subjected to criticism from a dissident minority. Conversely, many psalms describe the narrator as being hounded by a crowd, without any provocation on his part—

MSB: Whereas Nietzsche, notably in *The Antichrist*, interprets the minority point of view in psychological terms.

RG: Yes, he restores myth to a position of honor. But Nietzsche's account should be seen as an explanation rather than as an interpretation. One has a choice, to take the point of view either of the victim or of the lynchers. And Nietzsche takes the point of view of the lynchers, as if it were the point of view of a small number, of an elite. This is altogether absurd: lynchings are the work of a crowd, of a great number. It is here that the Gospels exhibit their decisive originality. Not only do they not follow the crowd in condemning the victim, but the importance of the recalcitrant minority is emphasized by the role played by the eleven faithful apostles in the Gospels. We know the names, and almost the faces, of those who made up the minority. A further novelty of the New Testament texts in this regard, by comparison with those of the Old Testament, resides in the explicit presence of this minority, this minority of truthful witnesses. To write the book of Job, for example, someone was needed who was not like Job's "friends"—but there is no trace of such a person in the text that has come down to us.

MSB: No doubt we'll come back to Nietzsche a little later on. For the moment I'd like to ask you how the gospel phrase that furnishes the title of your last book is to be understood. At first sight, "I see Satan fall like lightning" looks to be very optimistic. It seems almost as though you're saying that Satan drops dead because he is struck by lightning.

RG: Satan is not necessarily destroyed. He fell, but he remains on the earth. In other words, Satan was transcendent; he was a celestial power. Now that he has fallen to earth, he is no longer a source of order, only of disorder. Luke does not say that Satan was abolished. On the contrary, because of his fall, Satan is now much nearer to human beings. This is how the passage in Luke (10:18) is to be understood.

MSB: This passage suggests that Satan acts in the world as a transcendent principle of violence, as both its cultural and religious form. Is the idea here that Satan's struggle is merely a symbolic expression of human violence?

RG: The most illuminating phrase about Satan in the Gospels, it seems to me, is this one: "Satan casts out Satan" (Matthew 12:26, Luke 11:18). The Evil One transposes violence in sacred and transcendent forms. But it is important, I think, to understand that Satan used to cast out Satan; since the revelation of Christ, however, he no longer has the power to do this. Whereas earlier Satan had put himself in chains, by means of the victim mechanism, today he is unchained, no longer capable of binding himself. To speak in Lacanian terms (not something I often do, by the way), I would say that Satan is the subject of the structure. It is Satan who causes mimetic wiles to act upon the world, and who directs their operation.

MSB: If I understand you, then, you are saying there is no Satan, there are only satanic relations.

RG: Are you asking whether Satan exists, whether Satan is a real being? I follow traditional medieval theology on this point, which refuses to ascribe *being* to Satan. This is a logical and consistent position, but not an obligatory one.

MSB: Do you also follow Saint Augustine in holding that evil is a lack of goodness?

RG: No doubt it is, but I'm not sure I comprehend everything this implies. Satan is always a "lesser being," a parasite on order.

MSB: Might Satan therefore be defined as a parasite on an order that precedes him and that he must destroy in order to exist? Paul says that before the Law there was no sin.

RG: It may be that's what Paul meant. Christ is the only man to overcome the barrier erected by Satan. He dies in order to avoid participating in the system of scapegoats, which is to say the satanic principle. After his resurrection, a bridge that did not exist before is established between God and the world; Christ gets a foothold in the world through his own death, and destroys Satan's ramparts. His death therefore converts satanic disorder into order and opens up a new path on which human beings may now travel. In other words, God resumes his place in the world, not because he has violated the autonomy of man and of Satan, but because Christ has resisted, triumphed over Satan's obstacle. That might well be one theory of redemption. There is no single theory of redemption. There are other acceptable, perhaps even preferable theories, but the Church has never said, here is the only theory of redemption that conforms to orthodoxy. This is very interesting. A French theologian recently drew attention to the fact that no schema of redemption has officially been endorsed.

MSB: To come back to the question of the relation between law and sin: Christ destroyed Satan's ramparts, but what was satanic after the revelation may not have been before.

RG: Exactly. One might say that so long as violence was transcendent, the only transcendence was Satan. But one must distinguish between religion and satanic transcendence. Archaic religion did not seek to unite itself with Satan. On the contrary, it sought to hold the god apart; there is nothing of Nietzsche's mysticism in it. After the revelation, what had been legitimate in the archaic period no longer was. Satan's various attempts to camouflage himself, to both chain himself again and to break loose of his chains, now became properly satanic. The term "satanic" applies here only to a world that comes after Christian revelation.

MSB: Nevertheless your reading of Mark's text (3:23–24) shows that Satan was always at the heart of rivalrous relations.

RG: From the moment that Satan casts out Satan, it is no longer a question of rivalry: Satan has now become the god of *violence.* Even so, I do not conclude from this that archaic religions were satanic. Archaic religions were legitimate in their place and time; they became illegitimate only from the moment that their lie was exposed. Before that they were legitimate. This is an important point, which I have yet to fully work out.

Scandal and Conversion

MARIA STELLA BARBERI: Following the gospel revelation, then, human violence was unmasked and became a manifest danger, threatening to bring us down, to lay us low. This, I take it, is what you mean by the notion of scandal—the stone, or obstacle, on which the sinner stumbles—which you sometimes identify with Satan, and which in any case is essential to the development of your argument.

RENÉ GIRARD: Yes, the gospel text explicitly likens Satan and scandal when Jesus admonishes Peter, saying "Get behind me, Satan" (*Vade retro Satana*, in the Vulgate), because you stand in my way: "You are an obstacle to me. You are thinking not as God does, but as human beings do" (Matthew 16:23). Moreover, Jesus, as a scapegoat, perceived himself to be a hindrance to those who witnessed the crucifixion.

MSB: In an earlier book you dedicated an entire chapter to the theme of *skándalon*.[1] Scandal, the most typical of mimetic relations, glorifies the ambivalent character—both attraction and rejection—of human desire. And since scandal causes those who are caught up in it to stumble, always on the same obstacle, its obsessive repetition ends up propagating itself, like a real contagion.

My question is this: doesn't thinking of scandal as a stumbling block, as a forbidden object or something to be gotten around, require that a person distance himself from his model—his objectal model?

RG: Lacan uses the word "objectal," it seems to me. Psychoanalysts have always used it, I believe—

MSB: I'm a Lacanian without knowing it! Let me rephrase my question. In view of the prohibition against provoking scandal laid down by Judaism—a prohibition to which you ascribe the character of "juridical transcendence"— how did Christianity take the stone that the builders rejected and make it into a building block, a cornerstone?[2]

RG: This is very clear in Dostoevsky. One can even read Dostoevsky's novels in this light. At the beginning there is always a scandal between the characters; then the great main scene opens with a collective scandal—in *Demons*, for example, the party given by the governor's wife, a snob who surrounds herself with all the revolutionaries. The chief senses of the word "scandal" dominate the text, each in its own place, until the Crucifixion.

MSB: One thinks also, in *The Idiot*, of the scene of Prince Myshkin's epileptic seizure and fainting.

RG: Yes, this tendency to collective frenzy is quite astonishing—

MSB: A frenzy that often is the sign that something has changed.

RG: In *Demons*, Stepan Trofimovich is scandalous for taking part in the revolutionary conspiracy, and when he leaves the town a conversion occurs. This is both the height of disorder and a conversion, though of course at another level than the founding frenzy of archaic societies.

MSB: Might that be an example of the gospel conversion you mentioned, in which the stone on which the sinner stumbles is converted into a cornerstone?

RG: Yes—but since the cornerstone is the Cross, my chapter on scandal shouldn't come at the end of the book! I realized this too late, and didn't have time to put the chapter in its proper place.

MSB: The theme of the closing chapter of *Things Hidden Since the Foundation of the World* became the theme of the first chapter of *I See Satan Fall Like Lightning*.

RG: This spiral structure is a constant feature of my work. Lately, whenever someone asks me what I'm doing, I say that I'm trying to write *Things Hidden Since the Foundation of the World* in reverse, beginning with the omega and not with the alpha, since the omega is the key to everything.

MSB: And so do we know in advance what the theme of your next work will be?

RG: I'm coming back to the archaic, to the sacralization of scapegoats. Judaism, by "dedivinizing" victims and "devictimizing" God, imposed separation and absolute transcendence. In Christianity, God is once again a victim. He is a divine victim. It is therefore unsurprising that for Judaism, as well as for Islam, Christianity should appear as a regression, a return to mythology. In reality this is not at all true, since the victim is innocent, whereas in myths the victim is always guilty in one way or another. It is in this sense, I think, that the dogma of the Incarnation must be interpreted. It is not a case of dogma divinizing a man. The divinization comes from God: "And the Word became flesh and made his dwelling among us" (John 1:14).

MSB: This is the theological question of the Cross, which is at the heart of your essay "Mimetic Theory and Theology."[3] In an eschatological perspective, the Cross cannot be considered an expression of sacrificial violence, at least not if one wishes to avoid having to interpret divine will as though it were subject to the same mimetic mechanisms that operate on human beings. How, then, are we to interpret the connection between sacrificial violence, as revealed by the gospel texts, and the sacrifice of Christ, which occurs as part of a divine purpose?

RG: The connection is evident in the prologue to John, which explains the link between the sacrificial violence revealed by Christ and the rejection of this revelation by the world qua world. This rejection did not prevent certain individuals from receiving Christ and becoming children of God.

MSB: Do you mean that even the rational significance of the revelation is subject to the incarnation of God?

RG: Yes, certainly. The scapegoat mechanism literally cannot be revealed without Christ: either it operates on the world and unites everyone, so there is no one left to reveal it; or it does not operate and there are people left to reveal it, but there is nothing to reveal—for, in the absence of unanimity, the mechanism cannot function. The Passion eluded this impossibility. At the beginning, the disciples were caught up in a mimetic frenzy and betrayed everyone. There was no exception to the unanimity, no clear-sighted witness.

For anthropological truth to be unveiled, the Cross was necessary. It was the gift of the Spirit: only the Cross could make the victim's innocence visible, by causing the Spirit to descend upon the disciples. But the fact that this revelation took place on the third day is very important. At first there was unanimity: everyone was united against Jesus, even his disciples. One would have said that Satan had won his wager. But then, two days later, the revelation occurred. The fact that it occurred afterward allowed the disciples to understand what was happening. The unanimity of persecution began to unravel: the Holy Spirit gave the disciples the power to separate themselves from the crowd and to contradict it. This is why the Resurrection must be considered a revelation.

MSB: Would you say that knowledge of a purely anthropological truth depends on faith in the Resurrection?

RG: By all means. Raymund Schwager recently remarked that I regard conversion as a precondition of such knowledge. I maintain that knowing the emissary victim requires a certain kind of conversion, namely, that one has to come to see oneself as a persecutor. Take the two great conversions that come at the end of the Gospels, one before Jesus's death—Peter's second conversion, after his denial of Jesus—and the other—that of Paul—which comes after Jesus's death. Both involve an awareness of oneself as persecutor. Peter had denied Christ and Paul had persecuted the first Christians.

MSB: Is there another kind of self-knowledge, apart from realizing that one has persecuted others?

RG: I suspect not. At the same time one must recognize that the notion of a scapegoat is paradoxical, even in its most ordinary sense. Because we see scapegoats everywhere, we loudly denounce their oppressors. But we don't feel that we are personally implicated in the scapegoat mechanism. The scapegoat phenomenon is universal as an objective experience, and exceptional as a subjective experience. No one says: "Sorry, I didn't realize it, but now I see that I'm a persecutor." It would appear that everyone participates in this phenomenon, except each one of us.

Christ had foreseen this. You shall all be scandalized because of me, he prophesied.[4] And so it came to pass: Peter entered into the crowd and became a part of it. But there was no way of knowing how to break away from the crowd. In three of the four gospel accounts, Peter—alone among the disciples—comes to realize that he has himself played a part in sentencing Jesus to death, and begins to weep.[5] Only Luke, to emphasize the element of divine intervention, has Jesus cross the courtyard and look at Peter—a scene comparable to the conversion of Paul. Luke, in other words, wished to make Jesus's role in this matter explicit, which is to say to make grace explicit. Luke in turn reminds us of John, who has Jesus say, "it is better for you that I go" (16:7)—that I die, because if I do not die in this fashion you would remain captives of the scapegoat system, you would always believe in it. The supreme paradox of the Gospels is that the Resurrection, far from being the supreme mystification, as it is now almost universally interpreted, is the source of all demystification. It is the Resurrection that enables the disciples to say no to unanimity. It demystifies the violent unanimity that is always visited upon the victim. To fully acknowledge one's own role as a persecutor, one must realize that only the death of Christ, and with it the escape from satanic influence, made it possible.

MSB: Knowing oneself to be a persecutor requires that the satanic circle be broken, and the breaking of this circle requires that each one of us resolve to disavow persecution. It requires, as you say, grace.

RG: John says, at the very beginning, "[T]he light [Jesus Christ] shines in the darkness, and the darkness has not overcome it. . . . He came to what was his own, but his own people did not accept him. But to those who did accept him"—if only a little, halfway, as the disciples did—"he gave power [i.e., grace] to become children of God . . ." (John 1:5–12). As a consequence, not everyone profits from Satan's defeat, from the breach opened within his own kingdom; the salvation of humanity will not come all at once. Those who accepted Christ were able to become children of God. But since not everyone took advantage of this offer, it remains true, strictly speaking, that men did not accept him. Salvation in the intermediate, historical period was possible, though not certain. Human beings could profit from grace. The disciples returned, but they were very few. This was the result of grace. The whole problem of grace resides in this. Nowhere in the Gospels is divine favor deserved, and least of all in Mark. But the disciples are disciples all the same, even if they displayed a lack of intelligence up until the Resurrection. At that point a tiny spark is struck: they answer God's call. In this sense the "good thief" should be numbered among the disciples as well. A personal, existential relationship was needed. But it is not enough to say that the disciples received Jesus. It is not enough because they were all going to betray him. Even Peter failed to understand this—unsurprisingly, since God was intervening in a hostile world dominated by Satan. How, then, could God break the circle that Satan had closed? By doing what Satan takes to be impossible: by dying, rather than exploiting the scapegoat mechanism. Jesus himself chose to be a scapegoat. The passage in John I have just quoted makes it very clear that, without the death of Christ, there would have been no conversion of his disciples. They would have remained prisoners of Satan.

Christ's death represents the loss of Satan's kingdom: the Satanic circle is broken, and the truth and grace of Jesus can now descend on those who are not afraid of accepting it. The Holy Spirit, which is to say the defender of victims, acts first on Peter and the other apostles, telling them that Jesus is innocent and that they are mistaken. Subsequently it acts on other persecutors, showing them that they too are persecutors, making them see the victim's innocence. What we call conversion is, finally, the experience of the scapegoat becoming the subjective experience of the persecutor.

MSB: You speak of the paradox of the Cross—an expression that is traditionally employed by theologians.

RG: I don't like it, really, for I see nothing here that is contrary to reason. The paradox of the Cross is that it reproduces the archaic structure of sacrifice in order to stand it on its head. But this inversion is a matter of putting right side up what had been wrong side up since the beginning of the world: since the victim is not guilty, he no longer has the power to absorb violence. In social terms, the Cross is the revelation of a destabilizing truth. One thing is particularly striking. Even though the structure of divine revelation remains unchanged from the archaic structure of sacrifice, revelation in the Gospels is granted only to a small dissident minority, not to the persecuting majority. It is reserved to those who see, and this unraveling of unanimity prevents the other form of religion, the archaic, from establishing itself. We see this at the conclusion of the Gospel According to John, which ends on a discordant note. Christ provoked dissension among his listeners wherever he went, and particularly whenever a miracle occurred. Those who claim that there is no apocalyptic element in John are mistaken. It's true that it lacks an apocalyptic chapter in the manner of the synoptic Gospels, as well as certain sayings ascribed to Jesus in those books, such as "Do not think that I have come to bring peace upon the earth" (Matthew 10:34). But the idea that Christ came to bring war is also found in John, in Chapter 9, where Jesus's healing of the man who was blind from birth creates discord among the Jews. Thus, John says, "a division occurred in the crowd because of him" (7:43). The outlook for the world in the wake of Christ's revelation is therefore exceedingly bleak. But the affairs of this world no longer matter. Union with God takes precedence.

MSB: You say that the death of Christ produced a crisis in worldly affairs. Mustn't it also be regarded as a moment of crisis in the world's relation to God the Father?

RG: I don't think so. Whether one is Orthodox or Catholic, whether one accepts the *Filioque* clause[6] or not, the Father does intervene in the world. It is from Him that grace comes, the Holy Spirit, which was not accessible until the death of Christ. Only then could a bridge be established between the absolute power of God and Christ's disciples. But perhaps you were thinking of the "My God, my God, why have you forsaken me?" of the Friday of the Passion.[7] The sense of abandonment is especially pronounced in Mark, the Gospel of the absolute scapegoat. According to tradition, the Gospel According to Mark was really according to Peter. The author of Mark, whatever his name may have been, was surely closer to Peter than to the other disciples; and Peter's betrayal is more powerfully evoked in Mark than elsewhere, more vividly described, because Jesus was in fact forsaken, even by Peter. This is different from what one finds in the Gospel According to John. Indeed, in John, Jesus always remains in control of what happens. In the account of his arrest, for example, nothing surprises Jesus. The same is true of the account of his death throes, more terrible in both Mark and Matthew than in Luke, where the agony is downplayed. In John one sometimes has the impression of a highly stylized representation, where Jesus is almost a Byzantine Christ in majesty. The differences in nuance are rather important. Critics have detected insurmountable inconsistencies in these accounts, but their diversity is also susceptible to another, more positive interpretation. The human mind is incapable of apprehending so great a truth by means of one text alone; in this case, four were needed. The variation in perspective was necessary, it seems to me, because the human mind finds it impossible to conceive at once of Christ as a total scapegoat and as a divine being. Each Gospel—and this is the source of their strength, taken together—lays particular emphasis on one aspect of the mystery.

MSB: Is the Gospel According to Mark, by virtue of its being the closest to an anthropological perspective, also the closest to your mimetic theory?

RG: Mark is the closest to the anthropological moment, which is to say the moment when there is no God at all. The Greeks didn't much like its long lists of miracles, but you are right, Mark is incomparable in its ability to reveal mimetic relations. It contains all the passages in which the disciples are shown in an unfavorable light: in which they compete with one another, for example, to discover who among them is the nearest to Christ; in which they construct their own hierarchy; in which they scapegoat each other, as it were—all these passages have great power. Mark captures all these things very well.

Some critics oversimplify in making Mark out to be a rebel, a subversive. The idea is grotesque. They go even so far as to imagine that, if the disciples are mistreated in Mark's account, it is because he writes against the apostles and, as a consequence, against the Church. In reality, the Gospel According to Mark demonstrates that illumination came only from the Resurrection, that prior to this event the apostles were incapable of understanding anything at all. The whole theology is there already, but it's still undeveloped, very compact. Because while it is the most specific of the Gospels, Mark is also the briefest, the one that has the fewest theoretical interludes. From Mark—the Gospel of the pure scapegoat—to John, the gospel message is increasingly theologized. The accounts grow longer and longer as one passes from Mark to Matthew, and then from Matthew to Luke.

But to come back to Mark. When I was writing the chapters in *The Scapegoat* on the beheading of Saint John the Baptist and the demons of Gerasa, I came to realize that Mark was very rich in concrete detail. In the case of the demons, for instance, this account is the only one in which the unclean spirit says: "Legion is my name. There are many of us" (Mark 5:9). It is the unclean spirit who himself says: I am the crowd, I am the Roman crowd. Today it is believed that the Gospel According to Mark was written in Rome, but ten years ago it was thought to have been written in Antioch. Who knows what will be believed tomorrow?

MSB: The historical-critical method of biblical interpretation seems to be enjoying something of a revival. What is your opinion of it?

RG: I haven't read any very recent examples of this method, but I have great esteem for the work of the late Raymond Brown, who was at St. Patrick's Seminary in Menlo Park, near Stanford, for many years. Brown was a meticulous scholar. He wrote a book in two large volumes, *The Death of the Messiah*, surveying the whole range of critical studies that have examined the four gospel narratives in microscopic detail, from the arrest of Jesus up until the Resurrection, including the trial, the Passion, and the crucifixion.[8] While remaining completely faithful to the historical-critical method, this work nevertheless manages to uphold orthodox teaching, even if it does accept some things that seem to me very doubtful. Father Brown firmly endorses the view that John did not know Mark. I think he is right. His arguments are convincing. John clearly did not take from Mark certain factual details that are common to both. The traditions are independent of each other and the vocabulary seems to confirm the absence of any mutual influence. And yet the details are the same. Now, if one really wishes to discredit the Gospels, one must assume there was a unique source for all of them. The Greek used by Mark is the most impoverished, the most grammatically incorrect, and yet the most powerful from a literary point of view. And Mark is also, as I say, the most insistent of the four authors in seeing Jesus as a scapegoat. Take, for example, the two thieves who were crucified after him. In Mark they are both hostile to Jesus; in other words, there is no exception to violent unanimity. In Luke, on the other hand, one of the two is not subject to this dynamic. He is saved, because he recognizes the truth. He recognizes himself as a persecutor.[9] This does not happen in Mark; there is no "good" thief there. The idea that Jesus is a scapegoat for all humanity is present in Luke, but other meanings are superimposed on it and make it less obvious. If one had only Luke, it would be more difficult to see how little the disciples understood prior to the Resurrection. But with the Gospel According to Mark, there can be no mistake: before the Resurrection, the disciples did not utter a single word that was not foolish. Not one. But Mark's harshness has a theological rather than a polemical or political function. In no way whatever is it a satire of the disciples. It is a portrait of humanity prior to Christ's revelation.

CHAPTER 6

I Do Not Pray for
the World

MARIA STELLA BARBERI: It is clear from what you have said so far that mimetic theory is very well suited to interpreting the Incarnation and the Passion of Christ, respectively, as the demythologization of religion and the revelation of the innocence of the victim. But does mimetic theory have anything to say about the eschatological consequence of the Incarnation and the Passion, which is to say the entry of the righteous into a heavenly Jerusalem made possible by Christ's resurrection?

RENÉ GIRARD: There can be no mimetic theory of the Resurrection. The Resurrection is either an invention of religious propaganda or the source of truth. From both a structural and a dynamic point of view, the anthropological and theological significance of the Resurrection is so coherent that it is very difficult to imagine that it could be an invention. An attempt does need to be made, however, to connect the whole theory of redemption with the resurrection of Christ. This is precisely what I tried to do a moment ago. The kingdom of Satan is sustained by mimetic unanimity. It is this unanimity that the disciples succeeded in shattering thanks to Christ, which is to say thanks to the grace that issued from the Resurrection.

I should perhaps say a word or two about what this implies. If grace comes from God, in order to reveal the truth to Christ's disciples and to the world, it is not for an earthly purpose since what is bound to happen next will inevitably threaten to destroy the world, given that the people of this world are not going be converted. In the Gospel According to John (17:9), Jesus says, "I do not pray for the world"—that is, I do not pray for a world founded on the scapegoat. Now that the world is deprived of an emissary victim, what will people do? Now that Satan will no longer expel Satan, he will be unchained. An unchained Satan threatens to destroy the world. This is the message contained in the Book of Revelation. We must work to rehabilitate this message, which is not to be confused with the wild talk of apocalypse—of the world's imminent end—to which it later gave rise. The disciples rightly saw that the Revelation marked the end of the system of things of this world. But they got a little ahead of themselves. They thought that the world had been so profoundly changed by the death of Christ that the scapegoat mechanism would cease functioning immediately. In fact, not even two millennia have been enough for the influence of the Passion to really seep in, to penetrate men's minds to the point that this mechanism is disabled once and for all; for the non-guilt of victims to be fully recognized, together with the illegitimacy of persecution and, more generally, of regimes based on the exploitation of one group of people by another; in short, for all the systems of violence that have been breaking down for two thousand years to be exposed. The disciples' only error—which in fact was not an error—was to believe that all this could be compressed into an instant, that one could pass from A.D. 37 or 38 directly to the year 2000. Theologians today omit to mention the apocalyptic passages that are found throughout the New Testament. Without ever actually admitting it, they construct whole theologies without referring to these passages at all. They have excised them altogether, just as they have cut out Satan. The Apocalypse and Satan have both been expelled, never to be spoken of again.

Hans Urs von Balthasar saw this clearly, and in the third volume of his *Theodramatik* (1973–1983),[1] says that mimetic theory reintegrates and encompasses important aspects of the New Testament to which theologians ought to pay greater attention. But he also has the impression that mimetic theory regards Christ as a random scapegoat, whereas in fact Jesus was selected as a scapegoat for a very good reason. Christ provoked Satan by offering the Kingdom of God to mankind. Mankind, in rejecting this kingdom, found a ready-made scapegoat.

Christ tried to shatter this system by offering the Kingdom. But the historical-critical method takes pains to distinguish between Jesus, a decent, somewhat naïve fellow who espoused a utopian, but nonetheless uplifting, view of human nature—a line of historical interpretation first advanced by Renan—and the cunningly subtle minds who invented the theology that is now familiar to us. This is a wholly false way of looking at the matter, it seems to me. The link between the Kingdom of God and the Cross is direct: the consequence of rejecting the Kingdom of Heaven is the Cross. In other words, mankind is always free to choose. If mankind had accepted Jesus's offer, there wouldn't have been a Cross: mankind would have proceeded at once from this world to the next, the Kingdom of God, with no intervening resistance. Mankind is responsible for the misfortune that came from its refusal of the Kingdom. The historicist mistake is the result of a misunderstanding that is both anthropological and theological in nature.

MSB: Moreover, in the Gospels, the choice concerning the Kingdom of God is sometimes presented in very specific terms—

RG: Yes. One encounters a parable of the rejection of the Kingdom of God in Matthew, for example. It makes perfect sense that the Church should have put Matthew at the head of the Gospels, by the way, because the scapegoat phenomenon is forcefully described there and, at the same time, Matthew contains more theological exposition than Mark.

MSB: Historical readings often revive the charge that Christians somehow misused the themes of the Old Testament. In the course of your researches you have worked chiefly on the Gospel of Mark. Was this choice partly motivated by an interest in avoiding an overly allegorical reading of the Old Testament?

RG: In order not to betray Christ's revelation, one must always keep all four Gospels in mind at once. John is very important for the dogma of the Holy Spirit. In Luke there are magnificent and indispensable things, such as Jesus's encounter with the two disciples on the road to Emmaus. This episode is essential in trying to make sense of the Resurrection. Understanding the Resurrection means understanding the New Testament—and therefore the whole question of the victim. Furthermore, the relationship between the Old and the New Testament is intelligible only in connection with the victim. It is in John that one finds the most interesting things that the New Testament borrowed from the Old. For example: "They hated me without cause"[2] (the very definition of a scapegoat) and "They will look upon him whom they have pierced."[3] One must always place the Crucifixion in the context of passages that reveal the innocence of a victim, which is to say Christ's status as a scapegoat. This is the true prophetic link between the Old and the New Testament.

The splendid passages read out during Holy Week, such as the Tenebrae readings, are first and foremost psalms of the victim, surrounded by enemies, who awaits his lynching. One thinks in particular of the passages from the Book of Lamentations (1:1–14). These and other psalms turn mythology inside out. But the good apostles of the present day find this distasteful. "Oh, it's all so terribly violent!" they say. "The man who is about to be lynched makes demands. He is unkind to his lynchers!" As Christians, the Bible's critics want sufferings to be endured without complaint. But the voices of these psalms call upon God for help, asking God to strike down their enemies! The perversity of the present-day objection, that there is violence and nothing else in these passages, could not be more clear. What do these passages tell us? They tell the story of a man who is persecuted, who knows that he is going to die. He is alone. He is afraid. The evocation of fear in these passages is extraordinarily powerful. Doesn't the victim have the right to complain, to call for help? To call for help, obviously, is to call for violence. But the interest of these passages does not lie in the fact that they are violent. On the contrary, they urge the necessity of escaping from violence.

MSB: You've partly anticipated the answer to the question I wanted to put to you next, about the "imitation of Christ." A considerable part of the apologetic literature is devoted to explicating this expression, which was—and continues to be—a paradigm of doloristic readings of Christianity. Just as Jesus suffered most cruelly on the Cross, freely accepting the role of sacrificial victim (in the sense of a sacrifice demanded by the Father, rather than the crowd), so the good Christian, in order to prepare his salvation, must bear the cross of life.

But when you speak of the imitation of Christ, you refer to imitation of the Father and contrast it with the attitude of those "bad masters" who, claiming that they are liberated from the need to imitate any model, see themselves as being imitated.

RG: The relation to the Father is a positive form of imitation. Christ's suffering was not imitation. Christ was original in his suffering. This is a good reason to be against dolorism. But Christ says: Imitate me, because I am an imitator of my Father! Contrary to what the modern prophets claim, it makes no sense to say: Imitate me, because I am not an imitator. Nietzsche understood the ridiculousness of the modern teacher, posing as an individualist, who says: Imitate me! He saw what that implied, and said: Do *not* imitate me—because otherwise you put me in a Christ-like position in which I have no desire to be placed.

MSB: Since the publication of *Things Hidden Since the Foundation of the World*, have you at all changed your view of Paul, particularly in relation to the Letter to the Hebrews?

RG: It is generally accepted that the Letter to the Hebrews is not from Paul's hand. On the other hand, the letter is very important as an example of the way in which sacrifice was understood. One must always be careful to put these texts back in their spiritual context. And the context of this letter is complicated. The Letter to the Hebrews seeks to define the death of Christ in terms of the traditional practice of sacrifice, and proposed this formula: the last sacrifice. This sacrifice is very different from the others. It is mentioned in the letter itself (Hebrews 10:5–6), echoing the fortieth Psalm, the most extraordinary of all the Psalms. The letter puts virtually the same words in the mouth of Christ himself (speaking to the Father): "Sacrifice and offering you do not want; you opened my ears. . . . so I said, 'See; I come' . . ." (Psalms 40:7–8)—which means: if you wish neither burnt offerings nor sacrifice, there is no longer any obstacle to violence; from now on, nothing can stop it. The old system is finished. Accordingly, in order not to inflict violence, one must be prepared to submit to it. Everything is summed up in this idea.

MSB: When the letter speaks of a last sacrifice, in other words, it is perfectly in keeping with the logic of renouncing sacrifice.

RG: Yes. That is why, after a certain point, accepting death becomes necessary. The fortieth Psalm, which closely resembles the Servant Songs of Second Isaiah, reasons as Christ does: since you refuse burnt offerings, I must resign myself to suffering if I am going to avoid becoming a persecutor myself. There is no intermediate position between persecutors and persecuted; no way to stand back, to adopt the perspective of the anthropologist or the sociologist, who imagines he can look in from the outside without getting involved. And so, at bottom, what I argue in *Things Hidden Since the Foundation of the World* is that the idea of a non-sacrificial vantage point, from which everything could be judged, depends on an overly anthropological point of view. Anthropology is all very well and good, but it can neither step back from the questions posed by the Revelation nor avoid answering them. There is no neutral position, no third way between Satan and the Holy Spirit—

MSB: Which implies that the social sciences cannot be Christianized.

RG: If the social sciences were to be Christianized, they would no longer be social sciences. They would lead to an impossibility. There is no way out from sacrifice. There is no purely objective knowledge.

MSB: One has the impression that your thinking is increasingly informed by an apocalyptic conception of the world. Do you believe that history is complete, that it has exhausted all possible potentialities?

RG: My thinking has always been apocalyptic. I think that, after the Revelation, the error of the early Christians was just this, their conviction that everything was complete. Even though my own perspective is apocalyptic, I don't say that the end of the world is going to come tomorrow. Nor do I say that it won't come tomorrow. In this regard we are in exactly the same position as those who came before us: we simply don't know. We are not capable of foreseeing the creative possibilities that this kind of deconstruction—the deconstruction of the old sacrificial system—produces. I think that we must examine our history and try to see whether, beneath what has already occurred, there are not additional layers of phenomena waiting to be revealed; whether some aspects of life that used to be constrained by the old sacrificial system are not going to flourish, other domains of knowledge, other ways of living. Everything that the Passion undid in the cultural sphere might well be an opening, an extraordinary source of enrichment. I am certain it is. One must also keep in mind what Jesus called the "signs of the times."[4]

MSB: Christ's injunction regarding the compassion and charity owed to all those whom we are accustomed to think of as victims has assumed in the present day an anti-Christian sense.[5] The ambiguity of this injunction therefore typically leads to broader conflicts in which each person vehemently insists that he is a victim. Is it in this context, an apocalyptic context, that our age is to be understood?

RG: The concern for victims seems to me to be both a positive and a negative phenomenon. The error arises from ideology—the idea that everything is either good or bad. The revelation of the innocence of the victim is the true Christian insight. It flourishes today, but over the course of the past century it managed to become the motive force for new ways of manufacturing victims. Its effect has therefore been equivocal. This does not mean, as I stressed in my last book, that anyone should object to the invention of the hospital, medical care, or social legislation; at worst, these things may be insufficient or poorly administered. It is not these things that are in question, but the virtually universal feeling of being victimized, which finally cannot help but contradict natural law and the whole law that governs human relations: if it is prohibited to prohibit, then I can desire what my neighbor has and disregard the Tenth Commandment. Once again one finds oneself caught up in conflict, without knowing why.

CHAPTER 7

The Catholic Church and the Modern World

MARIA STELLA BARBERI: You see the Catholic Church as the prototype of Christian testimony. Yet the Church has often been criticized for acting as the guardian of secular law, the institutional sacralization of violence. I'm thinking especially of the Inquisition.

RENÉ GIRARD: This reminds me of an Italian friend, an American citizen actually, who used to say that the Church is like a trade union: there's no point belonging to an affiliate or subsidiary; one must belong to the strongest and oldest organization.

MSB: Many people have said something similar. Max Weber, for example, used to say that if you feel a need for religion, there's no point looking around for something new—just go inside a church.

RG: Christians shouldn't seek to be in step with the thinking of their time. But if they do, they are no more to be blamed for it than non-Christians today. The Christian world has successively been feudal, aristocratic, bourgeois, and, now, democratic. Imagine the burden of responsibility borne by the early Christians, suddenly confronted with Christ's revelation and the

rupture it caused with an age-old tradition of belief in the efficacy of violence. It is unthinkable that they should have instantly been transformed into
people of the twentieth century. True, they committed all sorts of misdeeds;
but these could be seen as misdeeds only afterward, thanks to a measure of
historical perspective that was denied them in their own day. The behavior of
the Church, in other words, is determined to some extent by the possibilities
of the age. I recall reading, in an American anthology, a very modern letter
written by the Spanish Grand Inquisitor in 1600 or so, taking a hard line
against witch-hunts. He saw the necessity of controlling crowd hysteria in
the name of the law. The Inquisition thus upheld the cause of jurisprudence
in attempting to combat populist excesses. Nowadays we no longer have any
need to put the Inquisition on trial; it's already been done. Nevertheless we
ought not forget that in the thirteenth century, at the time of the war against
the Albigensians—when the legate of Innocent III said, "Kill them all, God
will know his own"—it is because people really believed in heaven that they
said such things. They thought that to send the Albigensians to heaven or to
hell a little sooner or a little later wouldn't change anything. In any case they
believed that the law should decide, not the crowd.

MSB: That's not politically correct.

RG: Not at all. But think of it, making such a fuss over the Inquisition in the
twentieth century—an age that experienced Nazism and Communism! The
Inquisition has to be put on trial, everyone says. The Inquisition has been
tried in the media a hundred thousand times. But Stalin? Much less often.
French Stalinists? Not at all. History, I believe, has got to be taken seriously.
This business of treating everything as though it were on the same level is
possible only if you have lost all awareness of history—and this at just the
moment when it has become indispensable. All the sciences are now being
historicized, even astrophysics, which is seen to have obeyed the theory of
evolution no less faithfully than the others. For my part, I am seeking to show
the fundamentally historical nature of religion. We condemn the Inquisition
in the name of Christian values. After all, we can't condemn it in the name
of the *Mahabharata*, which is comprised of a series of alternating murders,
rather like the *Iliad*!

That said, the fact that the innocence of certain types of victims can be recognized is extraordinary. This is the power of our world. It is so strong that, instead of suspecting that something totally new is at work, we judge history as though people who lived in the twelfth century should be castigated for not thinking like readers of *Le Monde* or *The New York Times* today. In one sense, of course, we are justified in doing so: thanks to the revelation that was given to them, Christians ought to have been ahead of the others; but in fact we have all gone forward more or less together. Christians have therefore failed, and so from a historical point of view I think that the Pope is right to ask forgiveness. Conservatives will tell you that everyone failed. Fine, but that's not enough: Christians ought to have understood the holy scriptures otherwise than they did. No doubt there were some who did understand, but who had no say in the affairs of the Church. They didn't dominate Church politics.

MSB: That brings me my next question. Are we justified in speaking, in connection with the Catholic Church, of a contradiction between the institutional and prophetic aspects of religion, as Jacob Taubes and many others have done?

RG: People like Taubes speak of this institutional aspect as though the Church were still a major part of our lives—as though we paid a tithe every six months and heeded the rulings of ecclesiastical courts. But the Church no longer has any power. These therefore are phantom arguments made by people who do not wish to concern themselves with the realities of the present-day world. It goes without saying that the Church is also an administrative body, and that without an institutional structure of some sort there would be no Church at all—further proof of an institutional crisis, for in this respect today the Church is totally devoid of laws. The first millennium was the era of the great instructional councils. There followed a slow process of disintegration during the second millennium, beginning with the schism between Eastern and Western Christendom of 1054. Today, almost a thousand years later, we are witnessing the breakdown of the Reformation. There are now thousands of Protestant churches. Protestantism is coming apart at the seams, crumbling really. Yet some of the new churches display more spiritual fervor than the old ones.

MSB: It's important, I agree, to consider the present condition of the Church in historical perspective. The Church continues to be fantasized, mythologized, as it were—as if it were to blame for all the world's misfortunes. But do you see Christianity as having played some part over the centuries in bringing about the extreme disorder we witness in the world today? Is there anything exceptional about this disorder?

RG: When a question is important, it's important not to be mistaken about what is at issue. Catholics have very often criticized me for not having an ecclesiological theory, and in a way they have a point, because I am neither a theologian nor a student of Church doctrine. And yet one must defend the Church when it is made into a scapegoat, which I find all the more scandalous since the scapegoating has been done by Catholics themselves. If they understood what is at stake today, they wouldn't do such a thing to their own Church. This is really La Fontaine's fable of the lion grown old. The lion is now vulnerable to attack by all the other animals—but when he sees the ass coming toward him, he prepares to defend himself. For my part, I prefer not to play the role of the ass.

To come back to your question, I think that the legitimacy of the Church resides in its link with Christ. Paul, for example, saw this clearly. What seems to me most striking about Paul is that he found himself faced with the same problem in dealing with Peter that many people, in all ages, have found themselves faced with in dealing with Rome. Paul was more radical than Peter. He lectured Peter, and often strongly disapproved of him. But in the end Paul always gave into him because he knew that Christ had wanted Peter to speak for him. Paul went right to the heart of the matter in everything, and here he recognized the authority of tradition—a tradition that had only been in existence for a quarter-century! And it is because he was perfectly aware of what was at stake that he acted as he did. If he hadn't, Christianity would never have survived; it would have fallen apart at once. To understand Christianity and orthodoxy one must think of Paul. Paul was indeed stronger than Peter, better educated, more cosmopolitan, but he always yielded to Peter's primacy.

MSB: At a conference recently, someone asked in a rather exasperated tone of voice, "How can one still speak of René Girard after Auschwitz?"

RG: Let me point out, first, that there is a chronological problem here. How could one have spoken of René Girard *before* Auschwitz?

MSB: Right—how old would you have been?

RG: One hears the same sort of thing said about many people. It goes over well at conferences.

MSB: Seriously, though, what could such a question mean? That after the genocide of the Jews one cannot speak of any other scapegoat?

RG: In my last book I spoke of anti-Semitism and Nazism in the chapter on Nietzsche.[1] Instead of repeating myself, I'd rather refer the reader to those pages. And yet one may well ask what good a hierarchical ranking of scapegoats would do us. It would land us back in completely archaic models. The universality of Judaism comes from the fact that the Jews exemplify the experience of all peoples; that is, they resemble all the scapegoats of history. To ethnicize their position amounts to abolishing their universality. The entire meaning of Judaism is compromised if it is reduced to a set of local and ethnic claims in the name of multiculturalism. This way of interpreting the election of Israel is fundamentally wrong, I believe. On the contrary, Israel's election symbolizes a responsibility in relation to the universal. If one singularizes Israel in such a way that its universal dimension disappears, one does away with the very thing that is essential to it, thus creating a mimetic reversal of anti-Semitism.

Moreover, there is no comparable prohibition in the Anglo-Saxon world. In America every opinion is free to be expressed, however offensive it may be. Some years ago a neo-Nazi demonstration in a Jewish neighborhood in a suburb of Chicago aroused violent opposition, and the neo-Nazis had to be protected by the police in order for their march to take place. In this regard I feel I am rather American. Laws preventing people from speaking are regrettable. They never produce good results.

MSB: Do political, moral, and legal prohibitions against speaking of historical events function as substitute taboos for the ones our civilization has lost, or at least has very largely exhausted?

RG: It seems to me that it is always in the name of a greater humanity, of preventing people from being made victims, that measures of this kind are taken. But such taboos are directly contrary to the nature of revelation. People imagine that in treating scapegoaters themselves as scapegoats they can transcend archaic religion; but really they succeed only in falling back into its clutches.

MSB: Another possibility is that the question "How can one still speak of René Girard after Auschwitz?" simply identifies René Girard with Christianity. In that case wouldn't we have an excellent example of what you described in your last book, namely, a Christianity that's become a scapegoat for revealing all the things it has?

RG: Please, don't identify me with Christianity! But yes, I agree, Christianity now is the only possible scapegoat, and therefore the real unifying factor of our world. One sees this clearly in America, where the Supreme Court has prohibited all expressions of Christian faith in schools. Christianity is a particularly attractive target by comparison with other religions, to the extent that its universalism is more evident. I think that this tendency is going to be prolonged and accentuated, because the very things that encourage it are growing stronger. The totalitarian tendency for which the Church is reproached has been stood on its head. I see this situation as a continuation of the sacrificial system in modern times in a milder form, but one that nonetheless remains dangerous, and ever more revelatory as time passes. Moreover, paradoxically, a way out from our current predicament—aggregation, particularization, multiculturalism, and so on—can be found only by recognizing exactly this universal quality of Christianity, the only religion that can act as a barrier against these things, and therefore only by yielding to Christianity. I sometimes have the impression that Christianity is a last barrier, and that once it has been breached nothing will stand in the way of apocalypse. I don't see any other barriers.

MSB: What do you make of the attack on the pontificate of Pius XII, who is accused of not having spoken out against the genocide of the Jews? Do you think it is a question, here as in other cases, of taking a particular set of circumstances out of context and wrongly generalizing them in order to make the Church look as though it is guilty of persecution?

RG: I think it has to do once again with the attitude I have just described. It is obvious that the pope, in the Nazi era, was faced with a choice: either to secretly aid the Jews (a policy that he carried out while at the same time maintaining good relations with the Germans in order to preserve the papacy from destruction), or to publicly denounce Nazi misdeeds and to accept the consequences of doing so. He might very well have chosen the latter course of action. But he didn't, for many reasons. These reasons may have been bad ones, but they certainly weren't diabolical. It must be kept in mind that he was responsible for a great many people. He had also lived in Germany for many years and loved German culture, which exposed him to criticism.

MSB: But this is perhaps not a sufficient reason for convicting someone of pro-Nazi sympathies.

RG: No, not sufficient at all. The recent attacks on Cardinal Ratzinger are inspired by the same way of thinking.[2] Critics talk of the "dictatorship" of Cardinal Ratzinger! Have you met him?

MSB: I have—and, what's more, in an ideal setting, at the Sorbonne, where he came to give a lecture. I well recall his intellectual energy.

RG: Yes, he's a talented and thoroughly charming man. And yet for certain Americans he's worse than Eichmann, Goebbels, and Stalin put together. Imagine the courage it must take for men like Ratzinger to stand up to everyone else, to make themselves unpopular by reminding Catholic theologians that there are certain limits they cannot overstep if they are legitimately to call themselves Catholics. Ratzinger can't force anyone to do anything. After all, no one can be forced to remain in the Church against his will. Ratzinger does no more than repeat what the Church has always said. He also speaks frankly of his dismay at what is going on all around him. Think about it for a moment. What did he stand to gain from saying what he did? Was it really just a stupid error of judgment? That seems very improbable. The minister of the Church speaks in the name of the Church—a Church that today has no material power—because he believes it is his duty to do so. It's as simple as that!

At bottom, Catholics who confuse ecumenicism with a renunciation of the Church by the Church itself wish that it no longer existed. The Church has never been a scapegoat more than it is today. But one must see the symbolic value of this: whatever the Church may have lost by its compromises with the world, its enemies now give back by obliging it to play the same role as Christ. This is its true vocation. And now that it has been reaffirmed, it will enable the Church to shake off the indolence and decadence of the age that is now drawing to a close.

MSB: If what needs to be learned above all from Christianity is the true nature of violence, revealed by the historical figure of Christ, why then shouldn't we regard the current preoccupation with victims as the true fulfillment of the gospel message?

RG: Christianity is much more than this, of course. We aren't capable of grasping its full implication. But the defense of victims is an essential aspect, and one that is still being discovered in our own time. In this connection, Matthew's parable of the Last Judgment is incomparably rich in significance.[3] I would like to avoid speaking in terms of the forces of evil and the forces of good. I don't have the right to say what is good and what is evil. In reality, of course, the defense of victims may be a disguised search for other victims. I rather have the feeling that we are dealing here with an extraordinary combination of things—which is why I hesitate to blame those who take a stand one way or the other, even if their actions sometimes assume a rather doubtful form. One should be wary of saying anything peremptory with regard to personal involvement because there is no obviously right course of action.

MSB: We are in the process of becoming a globally unified civilization, with the result that obstacles to scapegoating are being swept away. At the same time, boundaries between states are our only protection in an age of globalization, and yet they too are increasingly weakened by the spread of violence. What role has this ambiguity played in recent conflicts, do you think? In the war in Kosovo, for example?

RG: Precisely. The case of Yugoslavia clearly shows that boundaries serve to contain violence, in the two senses indicated by Jean-Pierre Dupuy: boundaries repel violence, but they do so by violent means. To eliminate borders between states carries with it both a danger of war and a chance for peace— an additional degree of freedom that may lead to more evil or to more good. Here again one can do no more than express opinions. I'm inclined to take a rather conservative view: I see a role for national and international institutions in limiting violence; but the origins of violence are nonetheless to be found in sacrifice.

MSB: We need limits—and yet we need to transgress them. On the one hand, you emphasize the control that all religions exert over violence. On the other, you appear to be persuaded of the impossibility of escaping violence, of eluding scandal—as though it were built into human history.

RG: Human ambitions are, of course, contradictory. They assume various forms, each with its own share of violence. This is not without consequence. The term "scapegoat" is often used in the domain of labor relations, for example, but evidently this is not the same thing as killing victims.

MSB: Human beings imagine themselves to be more and more free, but they do not therefore cease to feel a need for religion. What can religion look forward to in the future?

RG: Obsolete religions are not going to be reestablished, because this can only be done in terrifying forms, such as Nazism. The more I read Heidegger, the more I am convinced that Heraclitus's concept of *pólemos*, the father and king of everything, is a pagan quasi-revelation of an original or founding murder. Heidegger had an inkling of this, but he associated it with actual instances of Nazi violence. He considered the neo-pagan character of Nazism as a measure of health, perhaps also of religious renewal.

MSB: The end of the Soviet Union portended a cultural transformation of the Western world, which is to say a permanent rewriting of history that is ideologically justified by a perceived need to align history with official, politically correct truths. This practice used to be confined to the USSR itself. But now it seems to be spreading, without arousing any moral qualms, without meeting any resistance anywhere in the world.

RG: In retrospect it is plain that Marxism expressed a humanist attitude that was at least roughly consistent with religious values. Marxism has now given way to a far more radical cultural revolution. This revolution has triumphed in democratic societies that seemed to have withstood the assault of Marxism by drawing upon deeper, more essential sources of social stability, in particular the family. These societies are now completely disarmed. The end of Marxism thus represents a new stage in the disintegration of the sacrificial order. Up until 1965–1970 or so, war still had a sacrificial effect. In France the change occurred in 1968, and everywhere else around the same time. Since then there have been only global phenomena.

MSB: But globalization, by stimulating a kind of defensive reflex, has revived a concern for local cultural identity and encouraged political aspirations that are as different from what globalism envisages as they are extravagant.

RG: In France this process began with the Bretons and the Basques, and, of course, the Corsicans. Jean-Pierre Chevènement, the Minister for the Interior, resigned his portfolio earlier this year because he feared that the terms of self-rule proposed for Corsica might spread elsewhere, by a sort of contagion. National sovereignty cannot help but be an important issue for government officials who are sworn to defend the country. It just now occurs to me that in France, for example, given the general anxiety today about consumerism, movements similar to the ones we are now seeing in Spain might spring up. One would expect that regionalism would diminish a country's influence in the world. The fact that it is spreading within European countries obviously strengthens the power of America. Outside Europe, the situation in Indonesia is instructive. Indonesia has no shortage of reasons for rebellion. But now all its 3,000 islands are in danger of going up in flames. Disintegration on this scale could occur anywhere except America. America is a different kind of nation. It has no regions, no really distinct regional cultures. What it does have is absolute social mobility. It seems to me that the Roman Empire side of America, the tendency to world domination, is growing stronger—as well as the necessity of combating terrorism wherever it may be found.

CHAPTER 8

Hominization
and Natural Selection

MARIA STELLA BARBERI: Some readers of your last book understood you to have given up on modern hopes and expectations of scientific progress. They feel that promoting research in the name of the future, rather than of the past, holds greater promise because it would open up new perspectives in mimetic theory. How do you respond to this suggestion?

RENÉ GIRARD: I think it is misguided. At bottom, what is at issue—and what has never really been discussed—is the capacity of mimetic theory to account for the process of hominization in terms of natural selection. I have given the matter some thought, but my ideas are not yet fully worked out. Darwin's theory remains a very fruitful hypothesis, it seems to me; certainly a great deal of work continues to be published. With regard to the emergence of those traits that set genus *Homo* apart from its primate ancestors, it turns out that later stages of biological evolution favored certain kinds of culture rather than others. Mimetic theory offers an elegant explanation for this, thereby filling a number of gaps in the standard account of hominization.

The point of view adopted by mimetic theory is totally different than that of nineteenth-century anthropology, which couldn't imagine that the study of animal behavior might be a means of understanding the mimetic reality that preceded mankind. People who criticize me for being stuck in the nineteenth century fail to see that mimetic theory is rooted in ethology. And it is exactly this incomprehension that makes the idea of a collective founding murder seem improbable to some. Obviously my thinking breaks with both German idealism and the post-idealism of deconstruction. It signals a return to reality itself, to the "referent" (a wonderful word, it seems to me). The linguistic nihilism of my critics conjures an image of tweezers, which they use to avoid having any direct contact with reality—even when reality is what one has to deal with. Cover that bosom, which I cannot bear to see.[1]

MSB: Two objections in particular have been brought against your theory in recent years. The first is social and psychological in nature. It criticizes you for having too negative and pessimistic a view of mankind, for claiming, in effect, that we can get along with our neighbors only by oppressing others. The second is theological, and reproaches you for seeing in Christ's sacrifice only the anthropological fact of communal reconciliation. From different points of view, these objections call into question the relationship between mimetic desire and the function of scapegoats. What do you say in response?

RG: They are not really objections. There are many people who don't like what I do. That's their right—no one, least of all me, forces them to read my work. But they completely fail to understand my purpose. I am first and foremost a researcher. I am not a French intellectual who proposes a certain way of looking at the new decade or the new millennium. I am a researcher, and what I have found seems to me to be true. I therefore don't feel obliged to modify my findings because more or less optimism is needed to satisfy some group of clients.

MSB: You are fond of saying that you are a Christian *and* a Darwinian thinker.

RG: It's absurd to think of the mechanism of collective violence as operating on the compressed time scale of human history. Once dominance hierarchies disappear, societies founded on them either disappear or embrace the sacred. Only the sacred can save them, because it alone can create prohibitions and rituals that eliminate violence. One mustn't think of archaic religion in terms of freedom and morality, but in terms of a mechanism of natural selection.

Richard Dawkins understands perfectly what the anti-evolutionists do not, namely, that geological time has nothing whatever to do with historical time.[2] In its initial phase, the invention of religion was intermediate between animal and man. My book *Violence and the Sacred* didn't pay as much attention as it should have to the fact that evolution operated over hundreds of thousands of years, which is to say a span of time that is absolutely inconceivable for human beings. If I could rewrite it today, I would try to show that, on an evolutionary scale, chance operates in a way that is different from the one we are familiar with, since death abolishes all "bad" possible outcomes. The scapegoat mechanism can be thought of as a source of "good" biological and cultural mutations.

MSB: In other words, it's the repetition of chance that creates historical time?

RG: Evolution always takes the time it needs. Billions of years to begin with, millions of years after that, then hundreds of thousands of years. But hundreds of thousands, millions, billions—these are all unimaginably large magnitudes. People don't understand the theory of selection because they compare it to the endlessly repeated copying of a text, in which every error, every new error—every "bad" outcome—is perpetuated indefinitely. But this is mistaken. In natural selection, all the "bad" offspring are automatically eliminated; they die off, leaving no line of descent. The only remaining outcomes are "good" ones. Some will nevertheless object that there aren't enough "good" outcomes, but this is because they don't understand what a million years means. Chance on this scale is not at all the same thing as it is over a hundred or two hundred years of human history.

Mind you, I don't say that this argument is correct, but surely it is plausible. Dawkins devotes a whole chapter in one of his books to the way in which bats navigate by means of a kind of sonar that tells them how far away an object is.[3] It is quite remarkable that only a few favorable mutations were needed for this auditory radar to develop as a result of natural selection. It was in thinking about Malthus's theory of population that Darwin came up with the idea of natural selection. Malthus had discovered a biological law according to which population grows faster than food supply, leading to ever higher rates of mortality. In the theory of evolution, these deaths acquired a positive sense since they serve, in effect, to rid society of "bad" outcomes.

Had this very simple point been made in *Violence and the Sacred*, the sense in which the founding collective murder has a positive character in relation to the origin and development of social institutions would have been clearer.

MSB: You developed this idea later, at least in part, in *Things Hidden Since the Foundation of the World*.

RG: Yes. The problem is figuring out what it explains. We know, for example, that human beings are self-domesticated by comparison with the great primates, the great apes, which is to say that the period of infancy in humans is quite protracted. Human offspring are born prematurely in the sense that they are dependent on their parents for a long time. Now, think of the advantage of an evolutionary explanation in relation to the domestication of animals. It allows us to see that premature characteristics are preserved in domesticated animals, as in humans, as a result of dependence, in this case on human owners. The rationalist thesis, by contrast, is highly implausible.

MSB: You are referring, I take it, to Bernardin de Saint-Pierre's idea that melons were made to be eaten at home with one's family?

RG: Exactly. Imagine archaic humans saying: "Let's take these animals home—after a certain number of generations, they will be better suited to our eating needs." This is most unlikely. Another reason must therefore be found. The true reason, I believe, has to do with sacrifice. Why did people keep animals with them? Surely in order to make sacrificial victims of them. It is sacrifice that taught human beings to eat meat, to drink milk, and so on. And it is sacrifice that led to the domestication of those animals that could be domesticated. These were nonetheless a minority. Take bears, for example. Obviously, as carnivores, they couldn't be tamed. But animals that could be tamed became objects of sacrifice.

MSB: So you're saying that chance, in the form of cultural evolution, operated over time to bring about the domestication of animals, which had been brought to live among human beings in order to be sacrificed?

RG: Yes. During the Vedic period in India, Hindus were very clear about the point of sacrifice. They wrote about it often and at length. The English scholars who first translated these texts in the nineteenth century were outraged. And yet the Hindus were right. In French one can read a short book (originally published as a long article in 1898) by the great Indologist Sylvain Lévi on the theory and practice of sacrifice in the Brahmanas.[4] Everything is there: doubles, sacrifice as a form of lottery, the creative character of sacrifice, and so on. The explanation of sacrifice, in the strict sense, is inextricable from the reality of evolution. Sacrifices had to be repeated over hundreds of thousands of years in order to produce sacred kings, animal domestication, and many other human institutions. All these things came out of sacrifice, just as the Hindus said. But how are we to convince people today that they were the result of natural selection? Zoologists and ethnologists agree that some combination of cultural and biological evolution must be assumed in order to explain the later stages of hominization. Even though hominization occurred over millions of years, it could not have achieved its present form without a kind of dovetailing between culture and nature. One of the main reasons for positing the existence of taboos and prohibitions is that human offspring, whose infancy had grown longer by comparison with other animal species, needed to be protected against the desire of males to mate again with females.

MSB: Can one speak of prohibitions among animals?

RG: Metaphorically perhaps, but not, it seems to me, in any literal sense. Some animal behaviors nevertheless do appear to be the result of a prohibition, for example, against killing the vanquished male in dominance contests. Why do you suppose a wolf who holds another wolf by the neck does not kill him, even though it is within his power to do so?

MSB: Because it is enough that the other one suffers. But isn't it precisely this social aspect that establishes and structures hierarchies among animals?

RG: Yes. Many recent studies on the great apes seem to confirm this. Konrad Lorenz long ago observed that when animals do not know each other, they are always ready to fight. Nevertheless they approach each other with a tentative, wait-and-see attitude. The result is either combat or friendship, depending on the other's response. If the response is positive, the dominant challenger turns his attention to some other animal, inviting his new partner to join him, to be his ally. This new animal may be a member of the same species or, indeed, of almost any other. I discussed all this, I believe, in *Things Hidden Since the Foundation of the World*. Lorenz, in any case, saw the triangle and sketched its contours.

MSB: And so you conclude from this that sacrificial resolution, which separates mankind from the other animals, was a crucial response to errors and gaps in the transcription and expansion of dominance patterns?

RG: It seems to me that the intensification of mimeticism acted together with the increase in human brain size to destroy these patterns. The result was an increase in violence that threatened the species. At all events this danger seems to have been responsible for the process of hominization. Only in humans, alone among the animals, did violence make victim mechanisms necessary and bring them into being. If original sin created the problem of violence, it found a solution in archaic religion. The paradox of human cultures is that violence expels violence: Satan casts out Satan.

MSB: Would you say that the advent of violence marked the beginning of humanity?

RG: The man of the Fall, fallen from grace, yes.

MSB: Fallen man being mankind?

RG: Mankind, period. There is no other man than the man of the Fall. In the beginning was the Fall. I believe I've already said that Christianity was made visible through sacrifice. Its genius consisted in just this, that it could, and in fact did, function in a sacrificial manner. One cannot fault either Christianity or human beings for this, because it was a historical phase, like the ones that preceded it. Christianity says so. Take Augustine, for example. He had a profoundly intuitive sense of mankind, perhaps because he was in contact with paganism. With the destruction of certain social structures, the like of his intuition disappeared. But all this is a question of emphasis. It may be necessary to lay emphasis on one aspect or another, depending on the period. Today there is a tendency to forget the deep anthropological intuitiveness of Christian tradition. This is why, from a traditional point of view, I probably represent an Augustinian reaction against an excess of humanism.

CHAPTER 9

A Stumbling Block to Jews,
Foolishness to Gentiles

MARIA STELLA BARBERI: Augustine's formula "victor quia victima,"[1] referring to Christ, construes the sacrificial visibility of Christianity in terms of a Sacrifice that put an end to all sacrifices—

RENÉ GIRARD: Yes, of course. That is also why those who are non-violent may implicitly (as the theologians say) be considered to be Christians. But they may be considered Christians in an explicit fashion as well, for often their non-violence is directly associated with this interpretation of the Passion. At bottom, then, non-violence is Christian. Have I already mentioned the Byzantine reading of *Oedipus the King*? The Byzantines interpreted Sophocles' tragedy as a Passion. They saw Christ in Oedipus; they saw the innocent victim. Francis Goyet, in his afterword to a recent French edition of *Oedipus the King*, rightly reminds us that the Byzantines interpreted all ancient literature as Passions.[2] One encounters these readings in the Middle Ages, where the king is always innocent.

MSB: The Middle Ages were very much concerned with the sacrificial; I mean, with those sentiments that, being linked to the sacrificial, are also the closest to the heart of Christianity.

RG: People then felt a need to ask more profound questions than we do today, even though they found it harder to conceptualize them. This way of experiencing Christianity is deeply Christian—notwithstanding that these people didn't believe, as we do, in the necessity of avoiding violence. After all, they wished to reconquer Christ's tomb in Jerusalem.

MSB: God is generally spoken of as author. Only in the Christian faith are author and actor thought to be such similar figures that we call them Father and Son. Does this unique relationship reduce the distance between God and the spectacle of a world filled with the noise of men?

RG: The creator par excellence, the Word, was beside God and nothing was created without it. But it created the world in such a way that, when human beings became intelligent enough to wonder about creation, they could remain atheists.

MSB: But if this distance, this gap, is impossible to bridge, does it therefore characterize the condition of fallen man?

RG: Here we are still dealing with the whole question of grace and conversion, which Raymund Schwager has very insightfully analyzed.[3] According to The Letter to the Romans, men may know that God exists, that the world was created, but they cannot foresee redemption by Christ since it depends on conversion. Thus the distance separating man from God can be bridged only through God's grace. Without grace there can be no redemption. Since men "know not what they do,"[4] there is no subjective experience of being a persecutor. A special grace is needed in order to know what one does, and only this grace can make us see the truth of Christianity.

MSB: At the beginning of our conversation, you said that the centrifugal structure of I See Satan Fall Like Lightning risked obscuring the successive steps of your argument. And it's true, the book does have a winding, spiral form—en escargot, as you put it. Isn't it exactly this that makes it easier to reinterpret the nature of sacrificial violence prior to the Cross, prior to the victimization of God?

RG: I hope so. The same idea could be put another way, namely, that the Gospels, because nothing is hidden in them, clarify mythology. Earlier I said that only the biblical scriptures can explain why mythic heroes are crippled. In return, the reading of myths permits a second level of understanding of passages dealing with Satan and apocalypse that are often forgotten by tradition, silently eliminated, as it were. If blindness and ill will prevent people from understanding the Gospels, going back and forth between scripture and mythology may help them to see that the Gospels cast light on the meaning of myths. This way of approaching the problem is very complicated, and still needs to be worked out more fully; but certain aspects of the rereading of myths in terms of the Cross seem to me to be very well treated in Giuseppe Fornari's new book on ancient Greece.[5]

MSB: The triumph of Christ marks the culmination of your work from a thematic point of view. But in the world itself, it also marks the culmination of the long journey of human violence.

RG: I think that Saint Paul's letters, particularly Romans and Corinthians, have the form of a mimetic spiral. Everything we've been talking about constitutes a sort of exegesis of what Paul had to say about the centrality of the Cross. The Cross is not only knowledge of God, but first and foremost an understanding of mankind. Paul was perfectly aware of this. It seems to me essential that the notion of the crucified Christ as "a stumbling block to Jews and foolishness to Gentiles" (1 Corinthians 1:23) be examined more closely. I had thought that Jacob Taubes, in his book on Paul's political theology, would develop this idea, but he never really gets around to it.[6]

MSB: Your acquaintance with Paul seems to have deepened over the years.

RG: I hope it has. In a way it is rather recent. I have come to better understand Paul through reading and talking with Protestants. Most Catholics speak mainly of the Gospels. Protestants, on the other hand, speak mainly of Saint Paul; they consider Saint Paul's letters to be the primary Christian documents. I would find nothing more interesting than to write on the relationship between Protestantism and Catholicism. True ecumenicism would be exactly this, understanding what the Gospels and Saint Paul fundamentally have in common. The anthropological interpretation of Satan offers an opportunity for going further in this direction, it seems to me.

MSB: You say that Satan was duped by the Cross. By this do you mean that in the aftermath of the crucifixion no historical relation, no opposition, can be imagined between God and Satan, between Christ and Leviathan?

RG: The idea comes from the first letter to the Corinthians, specifically the passage in which Saint Paul says that if the rulers of this world had known its consequences, "they would not have crucified the Lord of glory" (1 Corinthians 2:8). Why does he use such a phrase? Because immediately afterward these rulers understood that the main source of their power had been destroyed by the Cross: the truth about the victim mechanism was now revealed. Satan was not tripped up by a ruse of God meant to topple him from his throne, but by the fact that Christ was killed on the Cross.

MSB: And yet the triumph of the Cross did not settle the outcome of the struggle between Christ and Satan. You go on to say that God left room for Satan to manage the affairs of the world.

RG: In order to explain this to human beings, one would have to say: God leaves it up to you to decide. In other words, he isn't responsible for the fact that human beings get caught up in satanic entanglements. This in turn would have to be explained by means of one of Pascal's formulas, such as the one that speaks of God as a "hidden God," or Simone Weil's idea that "God withdrew." But if I quote such a phrase, I shall be rebuked by inquisitorial progressives for whom the only heretics left are people like me.

MSB: On the other hand, the Eastern Orthodox tradition looks to other passages, such as the one in the Book of Job (40:25) where God draws out Leviathan with a fishhook—a figure that seems to signify instead the idea of a continuous struggle, because the destruction is not total.

RG: Oh yes, of course—but the powers that be are clever enough to know that, once a breach has been opened up in unanimity, the way is clear to the total destruction of Leviathan. It seems to me that the phrase "I see Satan fall like lightning" means that although Satan lost his power to organize society, he did not lose his power to disorder it. Having fallen to earth, Satan can no longer be bound up in chains, can no longer establish the order of his own transcendence; he is now unchained, free to spread disorder throughout the world. This is the image found in the Book of Revelation.[7]

MSB: You're saying, then, that the coming of Christ, by fatally undermining the regime of violence, ought to have the consequence either that from now on heaven and earth are separate, ushering in the Apocalypse, or, to the contrary, that the immanence of the divine order, in the Hegelian sense, must now be considered to have been made actual?

RG: It's not clear. Sacrificial interpretations are always interesting, because they take into account what you have just said: they reflect the power of God in a world that, from the historical point of view, obviously remains pre-apocalyptic. Attempts will continue to be made, one after the other, to establish a divine order on earth. The error of idealists is to unfailingly believe that these attempts will succeed—whereas violence remains embedded in the world. The triumph of the Cross is the unfinished work of a tiny minority. Even if Satan is conquered each time an individual is saved, his power endures. It's my Jansenism coming out, you see. Satan has been conquered. But humanity, instead of bringing into existence the order of things that it desires, threatens to completely destroy the world instead. This order of things is historical. Luke calls it "the times of the Gentiles,"[8] which is to say the age of those who are going to convert, only in the wrong way. Ignoring the apocalypse of the Revelation to John amounts to converting to Pelagianism—you know, the theory of that old Englishman who believed in the excellence of the world and who took issue with the doctrine of original sin and of grace.

MSB: One should perhaps hope, then, that the braking force known as *katéchon* (literally, in the Greek, that which holds back or restrains) will continue to operate in the world.

RG: Of course—one wouldn't want to renounce *katéchon*! That would be to do away with everything else as well. But this is a totally negative reason for keeping it in force. I don't think a pure "science" of politics exists. A science of politics must try to defend order, to slow down the process of undifferentiation through the most peaceful means possible, while recognizing that it can aspire to absolute non-violence only at the price of unleashing the greatest possible violence. And since a true theory cannot be devised, the best one can do is to delay, to take the side of *katéchon* and try to strengthen its influence.

MSB: What difference, if any, do you think there is between a power such as *katéchon*, which postpones the end of time, and the scapegoat mechanism by which Satan casts out Satan?

RG: Whereas the Satan who casts out Satan well and truly represents order, *katéchon* is situated in a Christian world, in a world freed from Satan's rule, a world that wants no part of it. At the same time, *katéchon* still retains a little of the old order, without which nothing would stand in the way of absolute violence. *Katéchon* holds back violence, which is to say what is left once Satan has been cheated, duped. It must be admitted that, in order to prevent violence, we cannot do without a certain amount of violence. We are therefore obliged to think in terms of least possible violence. But, as a practical matter, it's difficult to say how little the least violence would have to be.

MSB: The effectiveness of *katéchon* is related to its visibility. This at least was the opinion of Carl Schmitt, who examined how it operates more closely than anyone else in the twentieth century.

RG: *Katéchon* is inevitably associated with a kind of knowledge, the knowledge that destroyed Satan. The old Satan, for his part, had a social—and, therefore, invisible—role. The question of *katéchon* concerns all those who have the authority to act. How must they act if they know? What is the weight to be given to sacrifices in a world in which the truth has been revealed? This is the modern predicament.

A complete answer to this question would in any case require an analysis of the extremely complex relationship between politics and theology. But I always quote Carl Schmitt when people criticize me for speaking of violence and crisis. Schmitt points out that the only science thinkers of the Enlightenment could imagine was a science of order. Furthermore, they denied that this science of order is itself order. For them, science could only be a discourse about order. And in this respect sociolinguists make a very pertinent point, that a discourse of this sort, even if it has been elaborated for centuries, may very well not reflect the truth. What Schmitt says about the Enlightenment holds for all the human sciences since, for anthropology as well as for law and political science. These sciences have never managed to come to terms with the phenomenon of crisis. And yet it is crisis that reveals who is in charge, who decides. To think about crisis properly one has to go back to a pre-Socratic notion of circularity. The thinkers of the Enlightenment never looked at matters from this perspective, because they regarded crisis as an accidental breakdown of order—something purely irrational that, as a result, could not be conceived. Here Carl Schmitt saw something of great importance for all the human sciences today.

MSB: In other words, they haven't managed to recognize the reality of disorder because they consider it to be nothing more than a momentary suspension of order—

RG: Mind you, this isn't acceptable from either the Christian or the pre-Socratic point of view. Take Anaximander's idea that human order always comes out of chaos and returns to chaos.[9] It bears on the reality of crisis. Did Schmitt speak of the pre-Socratics?

MSB: Not as far as I am aware, except in connection with the concept of *nomos basileus* found in a fragment of Pindar: *nomos* as king, as the chief religious or sacred means of delimiting and controlling violence. The limitation of violence is a fundamental theme in Schmitt's writings.

RG: Indeed it is, as for the whole German school to which he belonged. It had some remarkable thinkers—Walter Otto, for example, whose book on Dionysus appeared in Germany in 1933.[10] Otto stands opposed in this respect to the French Hellenist Jean-Pierre Vernant, who is incapable of seeing anything other than the "normal." Vernant finds the very idea of disorder absolutely shocking. He's just written an essay on Tocqueville that I would like to read. If ever there was a mimetic author, it's Tocqueville; and if there is a true science of politics, it begins with Tocqueville. It's only in the second volume of *Democracy in America* that Tocqueville really comes into his own, by the way. He was the first to perceive the difference between democracy and monarchy, which he rightly saw as being based on a unique kind of sacrificial animal, the king. Democracy, although it contains as many obstacles as there are individuals in society, leads people to believe that there are no more obstacles, because the king has been overthrown. No one before Tocqueville saw that, to the contrary, if the shadow of the cripple is no longer cast over the world, it is because the world is on its way to becoming a cemetery.

MSB: Tocqueville, the great prophet of modernity, was nevertheless vanquished. But the history of the vanquished no longer interests anyone today; it's the history of peoples who have no history that commands everyone's attention. The historian recounts the history of those who have no history, of victims who have no posterity—

RG: And in any case recounts it against himself, as a historian. Classical historians took an interest in certain Christian victims. The martyrs, for example, were considered to be important because they created a world that lived on after them. But today, neither the history of the vanquished nor the history of the victors has any interest. The victories of Louis XIV celebrated by Racine and Boileau are forgotten, having given way only to nameless victims, to the anonymous crowds of history.

MSB: More than anything else, it's a way of situating oneself in a non-history. Mimeticism taught everyone how to place himself outside history.

RG: Obviously it's the definition of history that is at stake. For quite a while now an attempt has been made to erase any distinction between history and ethnology. In France, the merger between the two disciplines began in the '1930s with the work of the Annales school on daily life and the history of customs and mentalities, which succeeded in abolishing the meaning of both. This was another form of undifferentiation.

MSB: You have sometimes said—for example, in *Quand ces choses commenceront*[11]—that the importance of political power is matched only by its impotence. What role do you think politics plays in the contemporary world?

RG: It plays a less and less important role, exactly. The point also needs to be made that the modern economy has a katechontic character, because it satisfies human wants. People say, we all want the same thing; and the economy says, you shall all have the same thing. This response satisfied people for a time. But they have begun to feel that the consumer society is no longer quite what it once was, especially since the last world war. Today, a rising living standard no longer gives people a sense of fulfillment—a little like the rise in the general level of neurosis.

MSB: Is the economy the *katéchon* of our world?

RG: This is what Dupuy and Dumouchel argue in *L'enfer des choses*,[12] even if they state the idea quite differently. In the United States it is plain to see. Computers are good for the economy, they're new. But Americans wonder, uneasily, what will replace computers. Mimetic desire is satisfied only for a time, which grows ever shorter. New toys must always be found, and that's getting harder and harder to do.

CHAPTER 10

Lévi-Strauss
on Collective Murder

MARIA STELLA BARBERI: What led you to take an interest in anthropology after the publication in France of *Deceit, Desire, and the Novel* in 1961?

RENÉ GIRARD: The book you mention dealt with a number of European novelists whose work had revealed the workings of desire and mimetic rivalry to me. When I was done writing it I began to wonder whether this desire is truly universal, whether traces of it could be found in non-Western and archaic cultures. I therefore set out to read the classics of ethnology. Before long I was simply overwhelmed by mimetic discoveries—I didn't even know how to go about organizing my notes. It took me about ten years to formulate the theory of collective murder, of collective violence. Still today I have an extraordinarily vivid recollection of these years, one of the best times of my intellectual life. It seemed I was constantly discovering things that had never been described before, without knowing how to put them into words myself. *Violence and the Sacred*, my second book, came out only in 1972, almost twelve years after the first.

These were thrilling but nonetheless difficult years for me. Another thing that pushed me toward anthropology was Claude Lévi-Strauss's books, not yet classics but well on their way. I learned a great deal from them. The first volume of *Structural Anthropology* had come out in 1958, and *The Savage Mind* appeared four years later. The existentialist vogue had passed, but its influence continued to be felt. Lévi-Strauss was often criticized, quite wrongly in my view, for being too dry, for dehumanizing everything he touched. His great book on the elementary structures of kinship, published in 1948, is unquestionably austere and rather technical, but what came after is as poetic as it is true. Lévi-Strauss is one of the great poets of ethnology. By immersing his readers in a wholly foreign world, he allows them to penetrate the mysteries of the primitive mind. His work has done more to change our way of looking at things than the realistic accounts of nineteenth-century anthropologists. And this was not the result of any sort of stylistic trick, or of some subtle technique for producing a sense of disorientation. It was the result of patient inquiry on the part of a scientist who was also a great artist, working in the most traditional of all genres: lucid expository prose.

But ideas aren't the only things that excite the reader of these books. There are all the things that make them not only true, but also beautiful objects—the cover, the illustration, the layout, the typography. The overall effect is very restrained, yet luminous. And even if the line drawings are spare, they are useful to students. I think Lévi-Strauss deliberately tried to keep production costs down so that students could afford to buy his books. The masterpiece in this respect is the first Plon edition of *Pensée sauvage*. I've taken very good care of my copy, still in fine condition.

If I speak of these books as works of art, it isn't in order to disparage their intellectual content, of course. Their author taught me to think in terms of *difference*, in the sense of the term that has become very common in the years since but that, to begin with, was his alone. This way of thinking is a vocation in and of itself, and for all sorts of reasons, mainly (but not exclusively) intellectual, Lévi-Strauss gave himself up to it entirely. It is certainly inexhaustible, as his work clearly shows. But it was also, for Lévi-Strauss, more than a way of thinking; it was a style of life, amounting even to a kind of asceticism. It permitted him not only to hold himself aloof from all the awful whining and moaning in the media throughout the interminable postwar period, but also—a supreme luxury, this—to make almost no mention of the extreme vulgarity of the contemporary world.

Because the subject that interests me most, violence, is at the heart of this unbearably maudlin comedy, there were bound to be quite a few rather inextricable misunderstandings, at my expense. In the eyes of many people, and of Lévi-Strauss himself, I'm afraid, I am a part of this comedy. I speak too much of violence not to sympathize with the droves of whiners who exploit it for their own purposes.

Now, when I said to you a moment ago that my interest in violence came from Lévi-Strauss himself, I was scarcely exaggerating. His work was very influential when I first looked into the subject in the early 1960s. I began by considering the role of twins in mythology, and suddenly I realized that in one of his books, I forget which one now, Lévi-Strauss treated a pair of twins the same way he treated all the other pairs of objects encountered in myths: he *differentiated* them. This, for me, was a kind of revelation.

To Lévi-Strauss's mind, what justifies the differentiation of twins is Saussure's famous definition of the sign. The sign signifies differences and nothing else; differences between this thing and that. Linguistically, there are only differences, even between twins. And even if identity does exist (Lévi-Strauss's followers told everyone a few years later that it doesn't), it doesn't really count for anything; it plays no role in culture, which is entirely a matter of language. As far as Lévi-Strauss is concerned, there is no such thing as identity, and this is why, faced with twins, he differentiates them.

I don't say that this attitude is completely false. Archaic cultures, like all cultures, seek only to create difference, and they never speak of identity directly. Nevertheless it would be wrong to suppose that they cannot speak of it. On the contrary, they hint at its existence frequently. One of the chief ways of referring to it is through the mythological theme of twins.

Lévi-Strauss was right in a way, I think, on a purely linguistic level, to search for difference alone. But on the level of culture, he was wrong. Twins in myth do not signify just another difference; they signify the loss of differences, which is to say identity. If cultures never speak openly about identity, it is not because they cannot. It is because they feel constantly *threatened* by it.

MSB: Why do they feel threatened?

RG: For the same reasons that all of us fear sameness, I suppose; for the same reasons that Lévi-Strauss himself feared it. Sameness is the terrible war in which twins are perpetually engaged, right up until the moment when one manages to kill the other—unless, of course, they kill each other first, as in

Aeschylus's *Seven Against Thebes*, and then it is pure tragedy; the contagion of mimetic violence has triumphed. When it spreads it becomes the famous war of all against all of which Hobbes spoke.

To reassure myself that I hadn't gone astray in trying to deepen the almighty doctrine of structuralism—and therefore in moving away from it, as I was later to do with deconstruction as well—I turned my attention to the tragic twins Eteocles and Polynices and the comic twins of ancient theater (we now have them only in Latin with Plautus's *Menaechmi*, also known as *The Twin Brothers*, but they existed earlier among the Greeks). These tragic and comic twins are the first, the most powerful, and in fact the only strong interpretation of the mythological theme, and they support a fundamental aspect of my theory, the idea of a violent process of undifferentiation, a mimetic crisis of culture.

The only way to think intelligently about violence, then, without becoming part of the slimy melodrama that dominates the airwaves today, is through Lévi-Strauss's concept of difference. It is in this sense that I am a Lévi-Straussian, in spite of what appears to be my anti-Lévi-Straussianism.

Twins are at the heart of the greatest literature because, unlike the social sciences, which understand only order (or rather, discourse about order, as Schmitt would have it), literature is a glutton for disorder, at least up to a certain point. To move an audience, a certain amount of disorder is indispensable.

MSB: Isn't the question of difference the very source of your disagreement with Lévi-Strauss?

RG: I wanted to profit from what is best in Lévi-Strauss without succumbing to the tyranny of difference that ended up engulfing the twentieth century—a very bad end, in my opinion. To look at things as I do, you have to begin by studying literature. Rather than clutter your mind with social science and philosophy, you're better off starting out with *Don Quixote* and *Notes from Underground*, not omitting Aeschylus, Sophocles, and Euripides' *Bacchae*. This is exactly what I did, and I was grateful for it ever after. It wasn't a deliberate strategy on my part, of course; chance wished it for me.

Literature made me understand that disorder and violence are the same thing as the loss of differences. Lévi-Strauss hadn't the least interest in such an education, of course, and one can't really blame him. But for him, and for the whole era that came after him, it meant ignoring the tragic, and even the comic; it meant shrugging off all the great problems that inescapably presented themselves in the second half of the twentieth century.

I remember being invited, sometime in the 1970s, I think, to speak at Yale, the capital of deconstructionism in America. Without suspecting for a moment that it might be considered a provocative topic, I chose to talk about Greek tragedy. Afterward the chairman of the department, the high priest of deconstruction in the land, asked me a single question, which wasn't really a question: "How can anyone still speak of Greek tragedy today, still be interested in tragedy after deconstruction?"

MSB: Wasn't this the famous Paul de Man, nephew of the no less famous Belgian politician, socialist theoretician, and Nazi collaborator Henri de Man? Paul de Man began his career as a literary critic during the war and sympathized with Nazism as well. At about the same time that his compromising wartime journalism came to light, the depth of Martin Heidegger's involvement with the same regime was first discovered. It was as though not one, but two, sticks had been thrust into the proverbial anthill at Yale.

RG: Quite right. And I hardly need to point out that it was the same story with Paul de Man's academic work—at bottom, very academic work—in relation to Aeschylus, Sophocles, and Euripides.

The most important moment of this period for me was when I understood, indirectly thanks to Lévi-Strauss, that the troubling identity of mythic twins is a metaphor for the conflictual collapse of differences, a source of infinite disorder. Greek tragedy makes this manifest. If twins are more frequent in myths than the percentage of twin births in actual populations would lead us to expect, this is quite simply because myths often resort to twins in order to say what neither philosophers nor professors of literature are prepared to admit, namely, that violence destroys difference, that mimetic crisis threatens all societies. Mimetic crisis sharpens oppositions—not by reinforcing differences, as the dominant ideology of individualism claims, but by emptying them of their content, by undifferentiating them.

Language manages to avoid being hobbled by the insufficiencies of the sign, even though it is based on the sign. It is symbolic in a sense that

Lévi-Strauss is surely better acquainted with than I. But on the point that concerns us here, differentiation, the obsession with language erects barriers that are only apparently linguistic. The long and the short of it is that it is much more capable of speaking the truth than contemporary nihilism is willing to concede.

The truth is that language transgresses just as it has always done, by defying all the prohibitions against differentiation with which it is confronted. Lévi-Strauss's own prohibitions are not as effective as those of cultures themselves; and even the most vigorous cultures end up falling back into the chaos made famous by Anaximander. The best-known surviving fragment of Anaximander's philosophy asserts that all things come from chaos (*apeiron*), and are then differentiated, which is to say they become things; but finally they all fall back into the abyss from which they first emerged, on account of their mutual, mimetic violence. As Anaximander puts it, "they give justice and make reparation to one another for their injustice, according to the arrangement of Time."[1]

MSB: You pay homage to Claude Lévi-Strauss while at the same time taking issue with his exclusive emphasis on differentiation, which you maintain needs to be examined alongside undifferentiation. Your analysis is more complete, for it is at once more ancient and more modern. But isn't there another bone of contention? It seems to me that Lévi-Strauss has spoken disparagingly of your work more than once.

RG: This is true. For my part, I cannot avoid saying rather negative things about Lévi-Strauss, but I wanted to make it clear beforehand that I do not minimize the importance of his work. Nor do I criticize his behavior where it does not concern me personally. I criticize Lévi-Strauss in connection with his criticism of my own work. Only a very few things are in dispute between us; perhaps nothing at all, in fact, if I am wrong in imagining that Lévi-Strauss has done me the honor of criticizing mimetic theory. My name figures nowhere in his work, and it may be mere presumption on my part to suppose that certain passages are to be interpreted as a veiled attack on what I have written.

Lévi-Strauss has been very careful not to read my work, I believe. Certainly he's gone out of his way to avoid making any direct mention of it. He seems to know me only through the intellectual rumor mill, which keeps him vaguely up to date. But he is surely not unaware that scapegoats and collective violence play a key role in my thinking—which leads me to believe that Lévi-Strauss was in fact referring to me in a quite recent essay written for a volume in honor of Françoise Héritier, where he expresses disdain for certain admirers of Freud's *Totem and Taboo*. He finds them doubly objectionable, because not only do they admire Freud, they also resort to the horribly vulgar idea of a scapegoat in analyzing violence. Lévi-Strauss's exact words escape me, but not their gist, and I can scarcely avoid thinking that they were aimed at me.[2]

Apart from the brilliant thesis of collective murder, which seems to me the greatest discovery of all regarding the origins of human culture, I have never found anything to admire in *Totem and Taboo*. Nor is Freud's crucial insight, which in any case can be detached from the rest of his argument, the source of my own hypothesis of collective murder. The origin of my hypothesis, as you well know, is the Crucifixion. Freud's theory and mine therefore have almost nothing in common. But Lévi-Strauss doesn't see it that way. It doesn't seem to occur to him that one can have a nuanced opinion of *Totem and Taboo*. Since I say good things about the book, he considers it to have contaminated my thinking. Lévi-Strauss isn't alone, by the way, in his determination to see me as an unconditional disciple of Freudian anthropology.

I do think Lévi-Strauss is perfectly right in saying that Freud cannot do what he believes he has done in *Totem and Taboo*, namely, provide anthropology with an authentically genetic theory, for he assumes at the outset, in constructing his argument, a set of propositions that can be derived only from the theory itself. This criticism seems to me correct—and I endorse it all the more readily as it not only has no connection with the mimetic theory of a founding murder; it also, inadvertently, demonstrates the force of my theory.

MSB: In effect, Lévi-Strauss makes a target of you, but it's a target he cannot hit because he doesn't know where to aim.

RG: He doesn't think he needs to read me since he knows better than I do what is, and will always be, the fate of those who become stuck in the cul-de-sac of *Totem and Taboo*. If I speak of collective murder in myths, it can only be in the way Freud does since I'm committed to *Totem and Taboo*. This is how Lévi-Strauss sees the matter, and he won't change his mind.

The point I wish to impress upon readers of Freud's book (a dwindling number today, it must be said) is that mimetic theory has nothing to fear from this sort of criticism. So far from undermining mimetic theory, it only throws its power into greater relief. Lévi-Strauss is utterly incapable of seeing that I have not set out to write *Totem and Taboo* all over again. My argument is elaborated from start to finish in such a way as to avoid the very rock on which, he thinks to himself with considerable satisfaction, I could not have helped but founder.

MSB: Exactly what place does collective murder occupy in your theory of the cultural evolution of human societies?

RG: My hypothesis of collective murder has nothing to do with the crime committed by the "sons" of a "primitive horde" who rebelled against their "tyrannical father." The murder I have in mind is a random and anonymous phenomenon that occurs between undifferentiated doubles, a phenomenon that produces mythological significance without presupposing its existence beforehand.

If I take the liberty of speaking of the genesis of culture, it is because a mimetic crisis abolishes all the mythological elements that encumber Freud's theory *prior to the collective murder.* This phenomenon is unleashed automatically, between anonymous quasi-twins, at a moment when all mythological elements have been destroyed; indeed, the mimetic crisis occurs before these elements even exist, in a past so distant that no document can confirm the genesis that I propose. However hypothetical it may be, the genesis that I propose is nevertheless theoretically possible within the very structuralist perspective developed by Lévi-Strauss himself.

There are indeed a few mythological elements that survive the mimetic crisis, so robust that violence fails to undifferentiate them through their destruction; and so ancient that they already existed among mammals, no doubt in a still more rudimentary form. Predators typically choose the weakest members of a troop of antelopes, for example, since wounded, injured, or otherwise disabled individuals are always easier to capture than healthy ones. Later they were to be found in human cultures, in the form of the archaic divinities—Greek, Hindu, and so on—to which collective murder gave birth. Human beings in search of scapegoats prey upon this same type of individual, which is why so many of the archaic and ancient gods are lame or crippled. The mimetic genesis of religion may be situated in the seemingly interminable transition between animal and man.

MSB: You said that Claude Lévi-Strauss isn't alone in making you out to be a garden-variety Freudian.

RG: He isn't alone, no. Before writing his contribution to the edited volume I mentioned, Lévi-Strauss may have read an article by an American scholar who, apparently in good faith, ascribed to me the exclusively Freudian idea of a single murder at the dawn of all human history—as if I had taken it straight from *Totem and Taboo*.

Perhaps Lévi-Strauss had read another recent article as well, this one by the well-known anthropologist Maurice Bloch, who, as I recall, pigeonholed me at once simply by attaching the epithet "Freudian" to my name.[3] As far as Bloch is concerned, I am a Freudian and nothing more, a mere Freudian; in other words, a classic Freudian—not even the slightest bit heretical around the edges.

The label isn't at all insulting, of course. But considering that the idea of collective murder is the only thing I have ever praised in Freud's work, and that otherwise I have spoken of the father of psychoanalysis only in order to attack him, and that I have often been reproached for this, the label is false. The next time Maurice Bloch mentions me, if he ever does, I wish he would show a little more imagination and preface my name with some other phrase—"retired cowboy," perhaps; or perhaps "Inca farmer," or "Korean dentist." I shouldn't think it would be too much to ask, because he is more interested in imagination than the truth. And it would make my life easier. The misunderstanding wouldn't be so hard to dispel.

CHAPTER 11

Positivists and Deconstructionists

MARIA STELLA BARBERI: From the anthropological point of view, there is a limit to our knowledge of ultimate things, a limit beyond which it is not given to human beings to glimpse the hidden foundations of the world. Hypotheses may be advanced concerning these foundations, but they cannot be known empirically. Nevertheless you insist, rightly it seems to me, that your work has the character of a scientific hypothesis.

RENÉ GIRARD: Mimetic theory does not pretend to be exhaustive from the anthropological point of view. It seeks to describe the transition from one type of religion to another. Beyond that, it does not claim to exhaust the innumerable forms this transition has assumed in human history. Whether or not it is right to resist the temptation to give a complete account of variants that hold no theoretical, no explanatory interest hardly matters, since a victim is always found at the center. Mimetic theory is explicitly anti-relativist, for it tries to give a unique and comprehensive explanation of archaic religion, just as positivist anthropology did. It doesn't try to do this in a positivist manner—though in some respects it doesn't disturb me to be called a positivist. Without entering into a technical discussion of what positivism involves, let me simply say that mimetic theory, the light that it shines on myths, explains too many things for it not to be true. As in a detective novel, when the clues become too numerous, they can't be regarded as the result of mere coincidence. Mimetic theory explains the presence of disabilities and infirmities in a great many mythical stories. When there is no ground for making a victim of someone—because he isn't guilty of anything—people act as children do and make a scapegoat of someone who is physically unattractive, or who is an outsider. The number of outsiders in myths is quite extraordinary. And why are so many victims lame? My work is scientific because it tries to solve the puzzle constituted by these clues, to explain why outsiders, many of them handicapped, are made into victims and forcibly expelled from a community. The burden falls on anyone who doubts my theory to supply a better explanation, or else to adopt mine for want of a more satisfactory one. Contemporary thought tries to avoid this choice by taking refuge in various forms of idealism. The fact that I situate myself in a scientific perspective is important for understanding my theory.

MSB: From a scientific point of view, the most probable hypothesis is the one that does the best job of explaining a given set of the phenomena.

RG: One may always suppose that there is another hypothesis that explains still more than the one that is presently accepted—but that, finally, remains a supposition. Karl Popper's claim that every scientific theory is falsifiable misses just this point. The fact that the Earth turns around the sun, and not vice versa, will never again be challenged. The same goes for the circulation of the blood. Here we have, rather than scientific hypotheses, something more like experimental results. When we see the sun rise, we don't imagine that it comes out of the Earth. We know very well that the Earth turns. In a certain sense it might be said that we see it turn. It is the same thing with witch hunts in the Middle Ages. What would you do if someone were to say that witch hunts were due to divine intervention? You would laugh at him, because you know perfectly well it's not true. You don't need a scientific hypothesis, because the evidence is incontrovertible. The fact that Jews were sometimes killed in the Middle Ages "without cause" is just that, a fact and not a debatable proposition. You're not going to wonder all of a sudden whether perhaps the Jews did in fact spread plague. The reason you're not going to has nothing to do with peer pressure; you know that you're dealing with a mimetic scapegoat phenomenon. Because witch-hunting is known to have been practiced in the fifteenth century, people instinctively leap to the same explanation that mimetic theory advances. But they run through the steps of the argument so quickly that they don't see the theory. They believe that they need only concern themselves with the "raw data" of conscious experience, and refuse to see that accounts of medieval religious persecution have exactly the same structure and the same themes as the story of Oedipus. And yet they do. One day the mimetic theory of mythology will seem as obvious and as natural as our spontaneous demystification of analogous phenomena in the Middle Ages.

MSB: Do positivists, in order to avoid inquiring into the relationship between fact and interpretation, and to be able to claim objectivity for their theories, have to become complete relativists?

RG: That's something I can't answer. But we shouldn't forget that positivist interpretation, in the most common sense of the term, very often illuminates basic facts. All the ethnological description that we possess we owe to positivist anthropologists. Without them we wouldn't have any information about archaic societies that have since vanished, leaving no written trace. The descriptions left to us by modern positivists—closely observed, very realistic in the nineteenth-century sense—are priceless. They have the same documentary value for us as Herodotus's *History* had for the ancient world, but they are superior to his account because they rely on myth to a much smaller extent. Even where mythical traditions are recorded, they are almost always outweighed by first-hand observations based on visual and auditory evidence. A kind of humility is needed, then, in order to acknowledge that vulgar positivism, as naïve as it may be, bequeathed to us a wealth of ethnological information that we will have to keep coming back to, because we don't have anything else to go on. These documents agree with one another too well for their accuracy to be seriously challenged. In other words, we are now in a position to appreciate what is really essential about the anthropology of the late nineteenth and early twentieth century.

Take James George Frazer, author of the celebrated *Golden Bough*. What didn't he understand about scapegoats? When he chose the expression "scapegoat" to designate a whole category of victims, he created his own categories, a bit tentatively in some cases, but he was always headed in the right direction. If he didn't get very far, it's because he didn't want to recognize the scapegoat in his world or in himself. Today we detect scapegoats in Victorian England but no longer detect them in archaic societies. That is forbidden. Frazer saw what the deconstructionists don't. He saw the scapegoat in archaic societies; he didn't see it in Victorian England. One might say that modern thinkers have been playing a game of hide-and-seek in order not to see violence: sometimes they see it in others and not in themselves; sometimes they see it only in themselves and not in others. In one way it makes no difference. But the fact that now we see violence in ourselves is a sign that the sacrificial crisis has become more acute. We may therefore hope that we are drawing nearer to the truth. The best way to prove the scapegoat hypothesis will be to look at people of the nineteenth century, who always found scapegoats in some earlier time, alongside ourselves, who can find them only in the present day. Bring the two together and you will have the truth.

MSB: How does mimetic theory go about doing this?

RG: Mimetic theory introduces the notion of evolution, of a break. It is obliged to take time into account in order to avoid anachronistic moral judgment. If you fully incorporate the notion of time, you aren't going to condemn archaic cultures. Our age is right, of course, to rehabilitate the scapegoats of the past—but we believe ourselves to be superior to our fathers, whom we have made scapegoats in our turn. We are like the hypocritical Pharisees of whom Jesus spoke, who sanctimoniously built tombs to all the prophets whom their fathers had killed, in order to glorify themselves.

MSB: Today, apparently as a consequence of the hopes for peace that are placed in ever greater undifferentiation, people consider the sort of fundamental inquiry you undertake to be politically incorrect. Unlike mimetic theory, deconstruction seems to transfer the properties of physical objects to objects of thought. Does this mean we are confronted with a last attempt to affirm, in a negative way, the self-sufficiency of philosophy?

RG: Your question deserves an answer worthy of the problem it raises. Mimetic theory considers undifferentiation to be a social phenomenon, and shows that it really does occur. From a positivist point of view, it is hard to distinguish between a differentiated and an undifferentiated society: in either case one is dealing with a state of human relations. Shakespeare demonstrated that the passage from a differentiated to an undifferentiated state brings about changes in social reality, and also that they are not essential. Instead they are a kind of mirror held up to the mimetic relationship between individuals. If this mimetic relationship takes the form of what I call external mediation, differences are unaffected. But if the mediation is internal, differences become unstable and begin to waver, signaling a drift off into chaos. In a sense, deconstruction may be thought of as a passive way of thinking once more about the state of human relations. Deconstructionists make the process of disorder, the loss of differences, absolute; they deny the social difference between people that is associated with external mediation. This is perhaps not philosophy's last gasp, only its most recent one—though it is plain that philosophy's resources are now almost spent.

MSB: Deconstructionists glorify the process of undifferentiation, while expecting this process to produce its own differences. But does the reluctance to inquire into the origin of differences result in a commensurate idealization of differences?

RG: The differences on which the deconstructionists insist are trivial, really. The reason they're unimportant is that they have nothing in common. The interplay of differences becomes entirely gratuitous, because it bears no relation to real violence, to anything outside the text. The common features of the Gospels and myths, by contrast, are so numerous that the differences between them become significant. But a deconstructionist would say: "Myths and the Gospels? A story by Maupassant is different from a story by Chekhov; but, in the last analysis, the difference between them can't be grasped." In short, there are only differences, for there is only undifferentiation. These differences make no difference. But explanation, if it is to have any significance, must have a foundation, an identity.

The reality of this foundation, in the case of myths, is impressed upon us through sheer repetition. So many phenomena couldn't possibly be presented in the same manner if there were no real victims underlying them. The similarity between myths and the Gospels is what allows difference to be real, what prevents us from treating them as merely equivalent interpretations. Analogously, if you look at accounts of the Dreyfus Affair, there is disagreement about who is to be blamed and who is to be declared innocent: the facts are all the same; difference resides in the assignment of guilt. Here we are dealing with an absolute difference, a difference that is part of the fabric of reality. This is what deconstructionism refuses to contemplate, because it considers that nothing is real, there are only interpretations. Accounts of the Dreyfus Affair are only accounts. But the Dreyfus Affair itself is a real phenomenon: the prison is real, and the accounts of this affair are true or false interpretations of a real phenomenon. What the deconstructors end up doing is getting rid of the common element that is rooted in reality.

MSB: Should the respect that you seem to have for the positivist approach therefore be seen as a reaction to the proliferation of subjective interpretations, accompanied by justifications that are every bit as subjective as the interpretations themselves?

RG: Exactly. Positivists think that there are only facts. Present-day Nietzscheans think that there are only interpretations. In reality, there are both facts and interpretations. And when Nietzsche said that difference arises from interpretation, he said something of cardinal importance for both myth and Christianity. But since, for him, only two mythic readings were possible—

MSB: And so the choice between them could only be aesthetic. But what interpretation is not arbitrary or subjective, a simple aesthetic choice?

RG: There are no sure philosophical criteria for judging between the one interpretation, which makes Dreyfus an innocent man, and the other, which makes him a guilty man. But this uncertainty does not discredit the Dreyfusard interpretation; it discredits philosophy. You know, when I say "false interpretation," "true interpretation," I am still thinking of Nietzsche, who saw that not all interpretations are the same. But he chose the wrong one, which is to say Dionysus rather than Christ. The deconstructionists, by contrast, though they have resurrected Nietzsche, want to avoid having to take a position on the issue of religion. The question that I put to them, then, is this: Do you agree with Nietzsche when he says that sacrifice, in the Dionysian sense, is necessary, and that the dregs of society must be eliminated? To be against sacrifice is all very well as a moral matter, but, unhappily, it is totally arbitrary as a philosophical matter. In fact, what Nietzsche called genealogy was the genealogy of Christianity. But he was able to trace this genealogy only by choosing Dionysus over Christ. At the heart of Nietzsche's genealogy is religion. In it one finds features common to both myth and Christianity, as well as differences between the two. It is always a question, you see, of the distinction between facts and interpretation. But in doing away with the religious issue, and the question of sacrifice, deconstruction avoids choice altogether.

MSB: Do deconstructionists avoid genealogy?

RG: They speak of genealogy in connection with all sorts of unimportant things—with everything except what really matters. Furthermore, as I say in my last book, it was Heidegger who gave them the authority they needed to ignore the religious concerns of the late Nietzsche. This was extremely clever. The idea of a "retreat from God" in Heidegger, as I understand it, stands in opposition to the "death of God" in Nietzsche. For Heidegger, the notion of God's death reminds us too much of Christ. He replaced it by what he considered to be the more subtle notion of a withdrawal, a pulling back from God. But Heidegger was also bent on removing the basis for Nietzsche's religious concerns. Indeed, he comes close to speaking of rivalry between Nietzsche and Jewish monotheism—mimetic rivalry, of course. This is at once a very profound insight and a very shrewd tactical move on Heidegger's part. And yet the rivalry is fundamental. It can't be done away with, because Nietzsche saw the essential character of the Bible in our world. At bottom, Heidegger either suppresses evidence of Nietzsche's intuitions about the biblical character of the modern world or dismisses them as superficial—

MSB: As if they were a mere psychological by-product of his rivalry with Christianity.

RG: Right, a deleterious effect of this rivalry.

MSB: In an interview a few years ago you remarked, with regard to the problem of deferring violence, that the idea that awareness of a looming conflict is capable by itself of postponing its occurrence isn't persuasive, and that Plato's work therefore isn't a revelation of the scapegoat mechanism, because philosophy is immune to it.[1] Am I right, then, in thinking that you regard the Platonic notion of representation—fiction, as opposed to imitation—as an evolved form of the archaic prohibition? In other words, that this is prohibition's way of immunizing itself against the violence unleashed by mimesis?

RG: I don't believe that merely being aware of the likelihood of violent conflict is enough to prevent it from occurring, no. It isn't consciousness that keeps violence at bay in archaic religion, but prohibitions, which are aimed at eliminating opportunities for violence, and rites, which, in furnishing violence with an outlet that is itself violent, only to a smaller degree, transform the most lethal violence into a less lethal form. Plato's famous opposition to poetry is in reality an opposition to the revelation of religious violence, in Homer and in the Greek tragedies. Plato sought to conceal violence, which is to say the power of sacrifice in its most moral—yes, moral—aspect.

In the modern world there are two main ways, philosophically, of dealing with violence: either one pretends violence doesn't exist, usually without knowing it; or, following Plato, who spoke about violence more often than any other philosopher, one tries to hide its existence. Plato, in spite of himself, revealed more about violence than all the others put together. And in uncritically taking Plato at his word when he argues against poetry, one fails to grasp the repudiation of violence that this implied. It is a mistake to suppose that he rejected poetry for aesthetic reasons. What is overlooked in all of this is that Plato came between an older tradition of philosophy and Christianity. He saw the danger of violence much more clearly because of his proximity to the pre-Socratics. The understanding of the danger is essential, vital in Plato. In this respect, deconstructionist commentary is of some interest. Derrida draws attention to Plato's loathing of religious violence and remarks that Plato does not use the word *phármakos*, the only one of its family not to figure in his work: all the other members are there except the principal one.[2] In pointing this out Derrida seems to me altogether objective and scientific.

With the pre-Socratics one takes a step backward toward mythology, a *Schritt zurück*. This is a necessary step—but only mimetic theory takes a second step backward and goes all the way back to mythology, revealing its true nature thanks to biblical scripture.

MSB: And Christianity?

RG: Same thing. Christianity does the opposite of Plato. The rejection of reality by philosophy today is the most astonishing thing imaginable. Perhaps it is the proximity of revelation, the ever greater pressure it exerts, that feeds this impulse. But I think that revelation is going to become obvious in the "end times," precisely because the Apocalypse marks the end, the pulling down of the mythological and philosophical screen that was erected against the truth. And since most people do not want to know the truth, this end can come about only in a violent fashion.

The truth of mimetic theory is unacceptable to the majority of human beings, because it involves Christ. The Christian cannot help but think about the world as it is, and see its extreme fragility. I think that religious faith is the only way to live with this fragility. Otherwise all we're left with is Pascalian diversion and the negation of reality. I've gotten interested in Pascal again, by the way. His notion of diversion, or distraction, is so powerful! But it's clear there was something missing in his life: he never had any trouble getting along with people. And even though his youthful brilliance aroused jealousy, he never experienced rivalry, even in science. As a scientist, he understood the importance of diversion, of distraction. But he never knew rivalry in love, as Shakespeare and Cervantes did, for example; he had no way of seeing, as Racine did, the negation of desire in the very functioning of desire. Bizarrely, this is characteristic of the great French authors of the Renaissance. Montaigne, for example, had no rival model. La Boétie, his best friend, died before any rivalry, any problem, could develop. Something was lacking, though to a lesser degree in the case of Pascal than of Montaigne, because Pascal was so profoundly religious that, in a sense, his faith compensated for it.

MSB: La Rochefoucauld says that Cardinal de Retz (whom he didn't like) looked upon Pascal as a great rival.

RG: The cardinal didn't have Pascal's genius, but he did have the human experience that Pascal lacked as both a very sick and a very lonely man. Montaigne, on the other hand, was too happy, too untroubled. Montaigne really prefigures the French bourgeois who has tasted success—the rat in his cheese, as one might say.

MSB: You consider Montaigne's carefree spirit as a form of social blindness. Do you see a comparable danger in the determination to experience love as the only thing, the last thing possible in life? One finds this determination embodied, for example, by Prince Myshkin in Dostoevsky's *The Idiot*.

RG: Prince Myshkin is an ambiguous, ambivalent character, and to consider him as truly good, as many people do, is an error. Looking at Dostoevsky's notebooks for *The Idiot*, we see that Prince Myshkin, just like Stavrogin in *The Demons*, is the hypostasis of a person who has no desire. The absence of desire is Stavrogin's weakness, his suicidal side. He makes all sorts of attempts to arouse in others the desire, the mimetic desire, that he doesn't have. This is very clear in the duels: he always wins, because he never loses his nerve. Myshkin's attitude is much the same, I believe. Dostoevsky himself, confronted with a personality that was stronger than his own, wondered if it was the result of an excess of desire, or of a total absence of it. His notebooks make it clear that Stavrogin and Myshkin are monstrous figures who lack the same thing. Like Stavrogin, Myshkin has a negative effect on people around him—General Ivolgin, for example. Women fall in love with him because he has no mimetic desire. They are therefore his victims, although Myshkin himself seems not to understand what is going on. Isn't this precisely because he is unacquainted with mimetic desire? It seems to be a kind of physical defect, almost a biological deficiency. Otherwise, Myshkin must be regarded as a kind of Buddhist. One character in *The Idiot* wonders whether Myshkin isn't carrying out a deliberate strategy. His attitude may well be entirely calculating, who knows? Dostoevsky himself, it seems to me, hadn't answered these questions in his own mind.

MSB: Isn't there something of this sort in Nietzsche's view of Jesus, who, in *The Antichrist*, appears as a sort of idiot?

RG: Nietzsche wanted to separate Christ from Christianity. He's not the only thinker who's wanted to do this. But against the view of Christ as naïve and unsophisticated, let me put the passage in Matthew I referred to earlier, where Jesus says, "You build the tombs of the prophets . . . , and you say, 'If we had lived in the days of our ancestors, we would not have joined them in shedding the prophets' blood'" (Matthew 23:29–30). Here Christ is denouncing the mimetic repetition of the past—the mimetic mechanism by which sons imagine they are better than their fathers, imagine that they do not traffic in violence. The same mechanism still operates today. It must be true that the Jews built false tombs for the prophets. This passage couldn't have been added to the Gospels. It couldn't have been invented by Matthew. Its psychological power is extraordinary! A naïve person couldn't possibly have said such a thing. Neither Myshkin nor Stavrogin could have said such a thing.

MSB: In contrast to the dominant perspective in philosophy and the human sciences today, could your method fairly be characterized as "rational realism"?

RG: Perhaps, but I have no certainty on the level of method and I have no philosophy. In a way, I don't understand the imperatives, the prohibitions of philosophy—for example, the rejection of reality we see today. Or, rather, I do understand them, but wanting to jettison emotion and personal involvement I find incomprehensible.

MSB: Isn't there a chance that the rational application of your hypothesis might create an illusion with regard to the formation of culture and society that becomes the common wisdom, just as deconstruction is in philosophy today?

RG: Perhaps, but it needs to be kept in mind that revelation enables us to go beyond the illusions of reason. When people get along relatively well with one another, they find it easier to enter into dialogue about reality, about the world in which they actually live. They can then come back to the great principles of reason. Look at the philosophy of Thomas Aquinas. Even if it doesn't address the paradoxes of which we've been speaking, for the most part it succeeds in getting at what really matters by applying a kind of Aristotelian and medieval common sense. Aristotelianism sees more important things than the German and Franco-German idealists of the nineteenth and twentieth centuries, who sought to avoid facts, real things. To my mind, being reasonable—rather than rationalist—means believing in science. Reasonable people have grown accustomed to treating "scientific facts" as objective features of the world that cannot be avoided.

Jacques Maritain believed this. Living as we do in a world that is so much more disjointed culturally than his was, we have good reasons to return to neo-Thomism. At the same time it must be recognized that, in philosophy, definitions of reason have no social character. Take Aristotle once again. Aristotle and people like him naturally had to be assured of protection in case the tide of popular opinion suddenly turned against them. As aristocrats, they could count on others to defend their interests. They didn't need to take matters into their own hands or to take precautions against the irrational behavior of the crowd. They defended reason, but they didn't see the threats that hung over it. As a consequence, their conception of rationality was overly optimistic. We would be wiser, I think, to define rationality in terms of the threats it faces on a social level. In particular—and this is what I've tried to say in the course of our conversation—the informative function of reason has no effect on the crowd, which is governed instead by the scapegoat mechanism. Either this mechanism operates as it should and produces unanimity, in which case witnesses are false witnesses, or it fails to produce unanimity and ceases to operate. The Passion is at once unanimity, against Christ, and the breakdown of unanimity—but it breaks down for transcendental reasons, for religious reasons. Neither philosophy nor political science has anything to say about this. Here divine reason regains its rightful place. It is the coming of the Holy Spirit that defends innocent people against persecution. But it must first be recognized that the Holy Spirit came for just this purpose, to protect them from becoming victims of violence.

MSB: Rites, institutions, and prohibitions in archaic societies have the function of establishing limits and boundaries against the spread of violence. This is what you call external mediation. But sooner or later fresh outbreaks of violence must be expected and, as a result, new conflicts among doubles. This is what you call the internal mediation of mimetic rivalry. Do you think that these two forms of mediation still have the same function in modern society?

RG: At the risk of oversimplifying a bit, I would say that external mediation works to prevent rivalry and all forms of internal mediation. This is what it did in archaic societies. But the prohibitions of external mediation, in order to be effective, must hide certain revelations. In modern society, by contrast, as prohibitions came to lose their force, internal mediation took over. Many people criticize me for no longer speaking of the difference between external and internal mediation. The fact of the matter is that I've never stopped talking about it, only now I use another language. The more Christianity made its influence felt, I believe, the more widespread rivalry and internal mediation became. Giuseppe Fornari's idea of "good" internal mediation is therefore very stimulating.[3] But perhaps it would be best to adopt a new terminology that would illustrate the two aspects of internal mediation, positive and negative, as it manifests itself in the modern world. My early books don't mention the positive side. It is only partially present in the ones that followed, and appears more fully at the end of my last book.

MSB: What direction is your thinking and research taking now?

RG: I would like to relocate my whole body of work in a fundamentally historical perspective. Already in my first book, *Deceit, Desire, and the Novel*, I had taken a crucial first step in this direction by emphasizing the historical character of internal mediation. But there it is described negatively, in a pessimistic way. A deeper historical perspective is needed. And as I mentioned earlier, I would also like to inquire further into the relationship between Judaism and Christianity. Jewish monotheism dedivinized victims and devictimized God. Christianity revictimized God. This is the triumph of the Cross, which I have put at the heart of *I See Satan Fall Like Lightning*. A certain number of things nevertheless remain to be said.

Finally there is the topic we talked about earlier, which is of great interest to me at the moment, the relationship between biology and culture. I've been reading the work of the late philosopher and theologian Claude Tresmontant. Tresmontant was a Christian, but his books interest me for what they have to say about genetic programming. He situates Christianity at the point of transition between genetic programming—dominant in archaic societies with regard to territorial defense, sexual and hoarding instincts, and so forth—and a new kind of evolutionary programming contained in culture rather than in genes. The argument is suggestive, but it needs to be developed further. Tresmontant doesn't take into account archaic religion, which he conflates with genetic programming in animals. Room has to be made for one more stage.

MSB: If, as you say, all institutions emerge from rites, does this mean that institutions are doomed to meet the same fate as rites, the same slow and inexorable loss of social function, the same violent degradation?

RG: I don't think so. Education, rites of passage, funerals, many of the practices of archaic religion remain viable in the context of the Christian world. They derive from sacrificial practices, but they can live on without them. In any case they constitute the only way for people to live together. Social life without rites is unimaginable.

Jehovah's Witnesses, for example, condemn Christianity for modeling its feasts on pagan feasts. They are wrong to do so, because the meaning of these feasts has changed. The evolution of humans from animals is an ongoing phenomenon. Its continuity is plain to see. The discontinuity of the Christian message, on the other hand, was not immediately apparent. As a consequence, we must take into account the continuity of history, and of the intermediate stages between sacrifice and the rejection of sacrifice. Claude Tresmontant develops these arguments up to a point, but without concerning himself with the role of sacrifice. He accepts the Cross because he is a Christian, but he grants it no real importance in this regard. He doesn't see that the Cross is essential.

MSB: This raises the problem of what you call "sacrificial Christianity."

RG: I still use the phrase "sacrificial Christianity" because it links the Cross with the events of our own time. Are we witnessing the advent of a new era of Christianity and of the Church, superior to the one we have known up until now, or will the present crisis be aggravated still further? There are clear signs of collapse, of disintegration within the Church. Are we going to live for a time without a Church? In one place Jesus says, "[U]pon this rock I will build my church, and the gates of the netherworld shall not prevail against it" (Matthew 16:18). And in another he asks, "When the Son of Man comes, will he find faith on earth?" (Luke 18:8).

CHAPTER 12

How Should Mimetic Theory Be Applied?

MARIA STELLA BARBERI: When you say that your ideas will either be rejected or become commonplace, do you mean that in the latter case they will be deprived of their interpretive force, or, rather, that in acquiring the status of a scientific theory they will become obvious?

RENÉ GIRARD: They ought to become obvious, because they *are* obvious! On the other hand, there's no shortage of ways in which they can be popularized, trivialized, turned into—how should I put it?—a kind of gadget. It's a good thing, then, that mimetic theory has never been fashionable. It was protected against fashion. Even so, it has made at least some impression on the popular mind. I notice that in France the expression "mimetic rivalry" is sometimes used as though it were perfectly familiar.

MSB: Did living in America help to shape your early thinking about mimetic theory?

RG: The literary critic Fredric Jameson thinks that my whole theory of lynching comes from my having lived for a year in the southern United States.

MSB: And you think so too?

RG: No, I don't. On the other hand, a writer like Faulkner is wonderfully intuitive in this regard. I don't much like reading Faulkner, I find his style tiresome. But his great novels, such as *Light in August*, contain a Christian symbolism that is equally well suited to scapegoat phenomena. Articles have been published on Faulkner and mimetic theory. In *Things Hidden Since the Foundation of the World*, speaking of truth in literature, I said that if you read what southern newspapermen wrote during the Jim Crow era, you will never find the truth; but if you read one of Faulkner's novels, you will find the truth. He shouldn't be criticized for having made sociology into literature. No doubt he wasn't the only one who did. But his insights are powerful, and truer than those of the social sciences.

MSB: Your early thinking about mimetic behavior wasn't a result of living in America then?

RG: No, I don't think so. Perhaps there were other influences. Certainly living between two cultures gets you to thinking, it detaches you a bit from one or the other. For example, I'm quite sure that Americans make Europeans scapegoats (particularly the French, because they're always so critical of America), and vice versa.

MSB: As someone who is not unaware of the risk that a model will become a rival, what advice do you have for those who take mimetic theory itself as a model?

RG: I myself am very mimetic. Since I'm polemical, I'm mimetic. I recognize that I'm polemical, and in my writing I need a kind of bait, a lure. Often it's the desire to retaliate that spurs me on, that makes me want to write. But this isn't very effective as a means of vengeance.

MSB: It may be effective as a means of motivation.

RG: As a means of motivation, you're right. Besides, all this is always mimetic, always.

MSB: And so your advice would be—

RG: To refrain.

MSB: And to renounce mimetic theory if one isn't mimetic enough?

RG: Yes, if one isn't at least a little mimetic. And yet why should I be giving advice in the first place? I have no business telling people what to do or what to believe. But if you ask me what mimeticism is, I will tell you: it's pride, anger; it's envy, jealousy—these are the cardinal sins. It's lust as well. Human sexuality is very important, because it's a permanent impulse, not something episodic or intermittent. There are no tranquil interludes in human life. Rivalry is what sustains desire. One finds the like of this among other animals. Take monkeys, for example, which are quite vicious and highly sexed in their own way. The mimetic analysis of sexuality contradicts Freud.

MSB: In setting an agenda for scientific research, what would you recommend?

RG: It remains to elaborate a properly mimetic method. This is exactly why authors such as Dawkins interest me, because they have developed an original and extremely suggestive method, one that is distinct from the method of history or of sociology; nor is it the method of zoology. But even assuming that a properly mimetic method could be worked out, I wouldn't dare go so far as to tell people what to do with it.

MSB: Not even tell them what *not* to do with mimetic theory?

RG: One mustn't think in terms of grand concepts—concepts devoid of human feeling. Everyone knows this, but it's hard to put into practice. The truth of the matter is that most people aren't really interested in mimetic theory. They are interested in the social ramifications, the moral implications. This is perfectly legitimate. But my interests are essentially intellectual, there's no doubt about that. Early on, people thought that I had a taste for violence. When I began to look at Shakespeare they urged me to write about *Titus Andronicus*, one of the early tragedies and especially horrifying in its

violence. Its popularity was a sign of the appalling taste of the period—
everyone said to me, you've got to check this out, it's really terrific. They also
thought that I was a great fan of violent films. Most people today, I think,
realize I'm a non-violent person. No doubt with age they've come to see that
what they used to think isn't true. What caused me to turn my attention to
violence was the hope of succeeding where nineteenth-century anthropology failed, namely, in explaining the origins of religion, of myths and rites.
All of which, of course, was meant to prepare the way for Christianity.

Notes

Chapter One. Violence and Reciprocity

1. Kathleen Freeman, *Ancilla to the Pre-Socratic Philosophers: A Complete Translation of the Fragments in Diels*, Fragmente der Vorsokratiker (Cambridge, Mass.: Harvard University Press, 1962), 19. For a stricter rendering, with detailed commentary, see Jonathan Barnes, *The Presocratic Philosophers*, 2 vols. (London: Routledge & Kegan Paul, 1979), 1:28–37.—Trans.

2. On the custom of ceremonial visiting (*kabigidoya*) and gift-giving, see Bronislaw Malinowski, *The Argonauts of the Western Pacific: An Account of Native Enterprise and Adventure in the Archipelagoes of Melanesian New Guinea*, 6.3 (London: G. Routledge & Sons, 1922), 163–66. —Trans.

3. I should make it clear that I myself am not an unconditional pacifist, since I do not consider all forms of defense against violence to be illegitimate.

Chapter Two. Noble Savages and Others

1. See Alfred Métraux, "L'anthropophagie rituelle des Tupinamba," in *Religions et magies indiennes d'Amérique du Sud* (Paris: Gallimard, 1967), 45–78.

Chapter Three. Mimetic Theory and Theology

1. See Raymund Schwager, *Brauchen wir einen Sündenbock? Gewalt und Erlösung in der biblischen Schriften* (Munich: Kosel Verlag, 1978; 3d ed., Thaur, Austria: Kulturverlag, 1994). [The present chapter was originally published in Józef Niewiadomski and Wolfgang Palaver, eds. *Vom Fluch und*

Segen der Sündenböcke: Raymund Schwager zum 60. Geburtstag (Thaur, Austria: Kulturverlag, 1995).—Trans.]

2. This quotation is taken from the English edition of Schwager's work, *Must There Be Scapegoats? Violence and Redemption in the Bible*, trans. Maria L. Assad (San Francisco: Harper & Row, 1987), 210.—Trans.

3. See René Girard, *Des choses cachées depuis la fondation du monde* (Paris: Grasset, 1978), published in English as *Things Hidden Since the Foundation of the World*, trans. Stephen Bann and Michael Metteer (London: The Athlone Press/Stanford, Calif.: Stanford University Press, 1987).

4. See Paul's Letter to the Philippians 4:7.—Trans.

5. See, for example, Paul's Letter to the Romans 13:1–7.—Trans.

6. John 8:44.—Trans.

7. Thus the rendering of *Paráklētos* in the New American Bible, at John 14:16, echoing the word's origins in ancient Greek legal procedure. Related meanings, preferred by Protestant editions, include helper, comforter, and counselor.—Trans.

8. 1 Kings 3:16–28.—Trans.

9. See René Girard, "Sacrifice in Levenson's Work," *Dialog* 34, no. 1 (1995): 61–62.

10. See François Lagarde, *René Girard, ou la christianisation des sciences humaines* (New York: Peter Lang, 1994).

11. See Ted Peters, "Isaac, Jesus, and Divine Sacrifice," *Dialog* 34, no. 1 (1995): 52–56.

Chapter Four. I See Satan Fall Like Lightning

1. See René Girard, *Je vois Satan tomber comme l'éclair* (Paris: Grasset, 1999); published in English as *I See Satan Fall Like Lightning*, trans. James G. Williams (Maryknoll, N.Y.: Orbis Books, 2001).

2. See René Girard, *Mensonge romantique et vérité romanesque* (Paris: Grasset, 1961); published in English as *Deceit, Desire, and the Novel*, trans. Yvonne Freccero (Baltimore: The Johns Hopkins University Press, 1965).

3. See René Girard, *La violence et le sacré* (Paris: Grasset, 1972); published in English as *Violence and the Sacred*, trans. Patrick Gregory (Baltimore: The Johns Hopkins University Press, 1977).

4. Also known as the Songs of the Suffering Servant; see Isaiah 41:8 and 49:1–13.—Trans.

Chapter Five. Scandal and Conversion

1. See the final chapter ("Beyond Scandal") in Girard, *Things Hidden Since the Foundation of the World*, especially 416–31.—Trans.

2. The reference here is to any of three passages in the synoptic Gospels: Matthew 21:42–44, Mark 12:10–11, and Luke 20:17–18; see ibid., 429.—Trans.

3. See Chapter 3 of the present volume.

4. See, for example, Matthew 26:31: "All of you will be made to stumble because of Me this night." (Here I follow the literal rendering of the New King James Version in preference to the paraphrase ["all of you will have your faith in me shaken"] of the New American Bible.)—Trans.

5. See Luke 22:54–62.—Trans.

6. The *Filioque* clause occurs as part of the third article of Catholic faith: "Credo in Spiritum Sanctum qui ex Patre Filioque procedit" (I believe in the Holy Spirit who proceeds from the Father and the Son). Upheld by Roman theologians, the clause was a source of controversy in disputes over orthodoxy between the Eastern and Western churches. See A. Palmieri, "Filioque," in A. Vacant and E. Mangenot, eds., *Dictionnaire de théologie catholique*, vol. 5 (Paris: Letouzey and Ané, 1913), col. 2309–2343.

7. See Matthew 27:46 and Mark 15:34, quoting Psalms 22:2.—Trans.

8. See Raymond E. Brown, *The Death of the Messiah: From Gethsemane to the Grave. A Commentary on the Passion Narratives in the Four Gospels*, 2 vols. (New York: Doubleday, 1994).—Trans.

9. Compare Mark 15:32 and Luke 23:39–43.—Trans.

Chapter Six. I Do Not Pray for the World

1. See Hans Urs von Balthasar, *Theodramatik*, vol. 3, *Die Handlung: Anlage des Gesamtwerkes* (Einsiedeln, Switzerland: Johannes Verlag, 1980). [Available in English as *Theo-drama: Theological Dramatic Theory*, vol. 4, *The Action*, trans. Graham Harrison (San Francisco: Ignatius Press, 1994).—Trans.]

2. John 15:25, echoing Psalms 35:19 and 69:5.—Trans.

3. John 19:37, echoing Zechariah 12:10.—Trans.

4. Matthew 16:3.—Trans.

5. See the chapter on the modern concern for victims in Girard, *I See Satan Fall Like Lightning*, 161–70. [There the origin of this specifically Christian ethic is located in Matthew 25:38–40. —Trans.]

Chapter Seven. The Catholic Church and the Modern World

1. See Girard, *I See Satan Fall Like Lightning*, 170–81.

2. Cardinal Joseph Ratzinger was elected pope in April 2005, taking the name Benedict XVI. Prior to this he was Prefect of the Congregation for the Doctrine of the Faith, which in June 2000 issued a document entitled "Dominus Iesus," later the object of much dispute, on "the unicity and salvific universality of Jesus Christ and the Church." As Benedict XVI he resigned his papal office in February 2013.—Trans.

3. Also known as The Judgment of the Nations; see Matthew 25:31–46.—Trans.

Chapter Eight. Hominization and Natural Selection

1. "Couvrez ce sein que je ne saurais voir." Molière, *Tartuffe* (Act III, scene ii).—Trans.

2. See Richard Dawkins, *The Selfish Gene* (Oxford: Oxford University Press, 1976).

3. The topic of echolocation in bats is treated in Chapter 2 ("Good Design") of Richard Dawkins, *The Blind Watchmaker: Why the Evidence of Evolution Reveals a Universe without Design* (New York: Norton, 1986), 21–42.—Trans.

4. Reprinted in a second edition as *La doctrine du sacrifice dans les Brâhmanas* (Paris: Presses Universitaires du France, 1966).

Chapter Nine. A Stumbling Block to Jews, Foolishness to Gentiles

1. "Victor because victim." Saint Augustine, *Confessions* 10.43.69.—Trans.

2. See Sophocles, *Œdipe roi*, with a postface by Francis Goyet (Paris: Librairie Générale Française, 1994), 137.

3. See Schwager, *Must There Be Scapegoats?*

4. Luke 23:34.—Trans.

5. See Giuseppe Fornari, *Fra Dioniso e Cristo: La sapienza sacrificale greca e la civiltà occidentale* (Bologna: Pitagora, 2001). [A revised and enlarged edition has since appeared under the title *Da Dioniso a Cristo: Conoscenza e sacrificio nel mondo greco e nella civiltà occidentale* (Genoa: Marietti, 2006), forthcoming in English translation from Michigan State University Press.—Trans.]

6. See Jacob Taubes, *La théologie politique de Paul: Schmitt, Benjamin, Nietzsche et Freud*, trans. Mira Koeller and Dominique Séglard (Paris: Seuil, 1999). [An English version of this posthumously published work, based on lectures given by Taubes in Heidelberg in February 1987, is available as *The Political Theology of Paul*, trans. Dana Hollander (Stanford, Calif.: Stanford University Press, 2004).—Trans.]

7. See Revelation 20:7.—Trans.

8. See Luke 21:24.—Trans.

9. Anaximander, fragment DK 12B1.

10. See Walter F. Otto, *Dionysos: Le mythe et le culte*, trans. Patrick Lévy (Paris: Mercure de France, 1969). [Previously published in English as *Dionysus: Myth and Cult*, trans. Robert B. Palmer (Bloomington: Indiana University Press, 1965).—Trans.]

11. See René Girard, *Quand ces choses commenceront: Entretiens avec Michel Treguer* (Paris: Arléa, 1994), 69. [An English translation, *When These Things Begin: Conversations with Michel Treguer*, was published by Michigan State University Press in 2014.—Trans.]

12. See Paul Dumouchel and Jean-Pierre Dupuy, *L'enfer des choses: René Girard et la logique de l'économie* (Paris: Seuil, 1979). [Dumouchel's contributions to this book will soon appear in English as part of a volume of his essays forthcoming from Michigan State University Press. —Trans.]

Chapter Ten. Lévi-Strauss on Collective Murder

1. Freeman, *Ancilla to the Pre-Socratic Philosophers*, 19. A fuller citation is given in the first chapter of the present book, which likewise deals with differentiation and contemporary undifferentiation.

2. See Claude Lévi-Strauss, "Apologue des amibes," in *En substances: Textes pour Françoise Héritier*, ed. Jean-Luc Jamard, Emmanuel Terray, and Margarita Xanthakou (Paris: Fayard, 2000), 493–96.

3. See Maurice Bloch, "Divine violence," *Le Monde de l'éducation*, no. 258 (April 1998).

Chapter Eleven. Positivists and Deconstructionists

1. See Markus Müller, "Interview with René Girard," *Anthropoetics* 2, no. 1 (June 1996): 3–5.

2. See Jacques Derrida, "La pharmacie de Platon," in *La dissémination* (Paris: Seuil, 1972), 148–49. [Whereas *phármakos* (poisoner, sorcerer, magician) is unattested in Plato, the related word for drug, *phármakon*, is found in several places in each of its opposite senses, healing remedy and poison.—Trans.]

3. See Giuseppe Fornari, "Les marionnettes de Platon: L'anthropologie de l'éducation dans la philosophie grecque et la société contemporaine," in Maria Stella Barberi, ed., *La spirale mimétique: Dix-huit leçons sur René Girard* (Paris: Desclée de Brouwer, 2001), 157–88.

Index

A

Aeschylus, 106, 107
Anaximander, 15, 99, 108
anthropology, xi, 26, 27–28, 103, 109, 115; mimetic,
    29–30; religion and, 31, 34, 72
anti-Semitism, 79
Aquinas, Thomas, 123
Aristotle, 6, 124
Augustine, 54, 90–91, 93

B

Balthasar, Hans Urs von, 68
Barberi, Maria Stella, ix, xi–xii
Bernardin de Saint-Pierre, Jacques-Henri, 88
Bible, 32, 33, 35–38, 49; Corinthians, 95, 96;
    Deuteronomy, 49; Exodus, 49; Hebrews,
    45, 71–72; Isaiah, 33, 51, 72; Job, 39, 51, 52,
    96; John, 40, 44, 60–64, 66, 68, 69–70;
    Lamentations, 70; Leviticus, 30, 33; Luke,
    53, 58, 94, 61, 64, 66, 69, 97, 126; Mark, 55,
    58, 62, 64–66, 69, 70; Matthew, 19–20,
    53, 57, 58, 61, 63, 64, 65, 69, 73, 82, 122–23,
    126; New Testament, 33–34, 38, 40, 49–52,
    60–66, 68–70, 117; Old Testament, 39, 40,
    42, 51–52, 69–70; 1 Kings, 42; Philippians,
    40; Psalms, 64, 70, 71–72; Revelation,
    68, 97; Romans, 20, 40, 94, 95; Solomon's
    judgment in, 42–43; Zechariah, 70
Bloch, Maurice, 111
Boileau-Despréaux, Nicolas, 100
Brown, Raymond, 65–66

C

Catholic Church, 75–84, 95, 133n6
Cervantes, Miguel de, 106, 121
Chevènement, Jean-Pierre, 84
Christianity: and ethnology, 22, 34–35; and myth,
    38–41, 59, 121; and sacrifice, 78, 80, 82, 90,
    93–94, 118–19, 125–26
collective murder, 35–36, 38, 86, 88, 110–11
colonialism, 35
competitive spirit, 7–8
conversion, 60, 63, 94

D

Darwinism, 35, 85, 87
Dawkins, Richard, 87, 129
deconstruction, xii, 86, 106, 107, 116–19, 123
de Man, Paul, 107
democracy, 75, 84, 100
Derrida, Jacques, 14, 120
différance, 13–15, 104–6, 108, 117–18

dolorism, 19, 70–71
Dostoevsky, Fyodor, 58, 106, 122–23
Dumouchel, Paul, 101
Dupuy, Jean-Pierre, 83, 101

E

Enlightenment, x, 26–27, 98–99
ethnocentrism, x, 21–23, 25
ethnology, 14, 22–23, 35, 38, 100, 103–4, 115
ethology, 86
Euripides, 106–7
exchange. *See* gift-giving

F

Faulkner, William, 128
Fornari, Giuseppe, 95, 125
Frazer, Sir James G., 22, 28–31, 115–16
Freud, Sigmund, xii, 4, 109–11, 129

G

genetic programming, 125
gift-giving, 12–13, 16–18
Girard, René, books: *Deceit, Desire, and the
    Novel*, 49, 103, 125; *I See Satan Fall Like
    Lightning*, 49–55, 59, 94, 125; *Quand ces
    choses commenceront*, 100; *The Scapegoat*, 65;
    *Things Hidden Since the Foundation of the
    World*, xi, 34, 40, 44–45, 57, 59, 71, 72, 88,
    90, 128; *Violence and the Sacred*, 23, 32, 49,
    87–88, 103
globalization, 4, 82–84
Goyet, Francis, 93
Grivois, Henri, 11

H

Hegel, Georg Wilhelm Friedrich, 97
Heidegger, Martin, 7, 83, 107, 119
Heraclitus, 7, 83
Herodotus, 23, 115
Hobbes, Thomas, 106
Holocaust, 78–79
Homer, 76, 120
hominization, 85–91

I

Inquisition, 75, 76

J

Jameson, Frederic, 127
Jehovah's Witnesses, 126
Judaism, 79, 125

K

katéchon, 97–98, 101

L

La Boétie, Étienne de, 121
Lacan, Jacques, 6, 53, 58
La Fontaine, Jean de, 78
Lagarde, François, 43
La Rochefoucauld, François de, 121
Lefort, Guy, 34
Lévi, Sylvain, 89
Lévi-Strauss, Claude, xi–xii, 14, 26, 30, 103–8; on
    Girard, xii, 108–11
Lorenz, Konrad, 89–90
Louis XIV, 26, 100

M

Mahabharata, 76
Malinowski, Bronislaw, 18
Malthus, Thomas Robert, 87
Maritain, Jacques, 124
Marxism, 84
Mauss, Marcel, 13, 16
Métraux, Alfred, 26
mimetic theory, ix, xi, 4–7, 15, 110, 113–17, 120–21,
    127–30; in human relations, ix–x, 4–11,
    107; and mimetic rivalry, 5, 7, 119, 124, 127;
    natural selection and, 85–91, 116; theology
    and, 33–45, 49–55, 59, 64, 67
modernism, 15–16, 100
Molière, 86
Montaigne, Michel de, x, 24–26, 28, 121–22
Montesquieu, Charles-Louis de Secondat, x, 26
multiculturalism, 24–25, 26–27, 31, 79
mythology, 32, 34–38, 50, 52, 59, 95, 110, 113–15,
    117, 120; twins in, 104–6, 107, 110

N

Nazism, 76, 79, 81, 83, 107
Nietzsche, Friedrich, 7, 35–36, 38, 52–53, 54,
    118–19, 122
"noble savage," 26, 28

O

Otto, Walter, 99
Oughourlian, Jean-Michel, 34

P

pacifism, 3, 19, 131n3
Pascal, Blaise, 96, 121
Paul, 20, 32, 33, 54, 61, 71, 78, 95–96

Pelagianism, 97
Peters, Ted, 44
Pindar, 99
Pius XII, 80–81
Plato, 6, 120–21, 135n2
Plautus, 106
pluralism. *See* multiculturalism
political correctness, 21, 25, 76, 116
Popper, Karl, 114
positivism, 113–15, 117, 118
pre-Socratics, 99, 120
primitivism, 26–31

R

Racine, Jean, 100, 121
Ratzinger, Joseph (Benedict XVI), 81, 133n2
    (chap. 7)
relativism, xii, 14–15, 34, 113, 115
Renan, Ernest, 69
Retz, Cardinal de, 121
Rousseau, Jean-Jacques, 26

S

sacrifice, xi, 16, 25, 41–44; of animals, 88; in India,
    88–89
"sacrificial Christianity," 126
Satan, 40, 51–55, 57, 62, 67–68, 95–98
Saussure, Ferdinand de, 105
scandal, 51, 57–59, 61
scapegoat: Christ as, 31–32, 33–36, 39–44, 50, 57,
    59–62, 66, 68–72, 93; Christianity as, 80;
    mechanism, 33–34, 40, 43–44, 60–62, 68,
    87, 96, 98, 120, 124
scapegoating, xii, 30, 31, 33–36, 39, 41–44, 59–63,
    68, 78, 79–80, 83, 109, 114, 115–16; of
    animals, 33; in Faulkner, 128
Schmitt, Carl, xi, 98–99, 106
Schwager, Raymund, xi, 33–34, 39, 40, 45, 60, 94
Shakespeare, William, 117, 121, 129–30
Sophocles, 93, 106–7, 115
structuralism, xi, xii, 106
Swift, Jonathan, 26

T

Taubes, Jacob, 77, 95
terrorism, ix, 4, 84
Thucydides, 23
Tocqueville, Alexis de, 99–100
Tresmontant, Claude, 125–26

V

Vernant, Jean-Pierre, 99
violence, 3–20, 25, 28, 29–32, 41, 50, 57, 82–83, 97,
    104–5, 120, 129–30
Voltaire, 26

W

Weber, Max, 75
Weil, Simone, 96